PAN–GERMANISM

DD119
U7
1913a

PAN-GERMANISM

BY

ROLAND G. USHER, Ph.D.

Associate Professor of History
Washington University, St. Louis

"The patriotism of nations ought to be selfish."
MADAME DE STAËL, *Of Germany.*

BOSTON AND NEW YORK

HOUGHTON MIFFLIN COMPANY

The Riverside Press Cambridge

121112

COPYRIGHT, 1913, BY ROLAND G. USHER

ALL RIGHTS RESERVED

Published February 1913

TO
THAT ENERGETIC, CAPABLE ADMINISTRATOR
THAT ENTHUSIASTIC STUDENT OF CONDITIONS
THAT BEST OF COMRADES
THAT DEAREST OF FRIENDS
MY WIFE

CONTENTS

vii

CONTENTS

PAN–GERMANISM

PAN-GERMANISM

CHAPTER I

THE CAUSES OF GERMAN AGGRESSION

FOR some years those at all familiar with current international affairs have known that it was the custom in the German navy to drink a toast, "To the day." Many people have hugged to themselves with glee the "secret" information that the officers were drinking to the day when war should be declared against England, but few indeed seem to have realized the splendor of the vision now before German eyes, or the ideas of the international situation which makes victory seem so near as to send German blood coursing swiftly in the anticipation of triumph. The Germans aim at nothing less than the domination of Europe and of the world by the Germanic race.[1] One of the fundamental

[1] "To Germany, a [fleet] is merely a means to an end, and that end — if the Pan-Germans may be believed — is the destruction of the British Empire, the disruption of the French Republic, and the domination of the world." Archibald Hurd in the *Fortnightly Review*, XCI, New Series, 785. Any one who will compare this article with the official Memorandum of the Admiralty prepared for the Dominion of Canada will have little doubt that it was "inspired."

errors, of which idealists and advocates of peace
have been often guilty, is to treat this vast project as an unreality. In fact, it is already half
accomplished. An equally mistaken view declares
it the conception of an individual which chances
to find for the moment a response in the German
people, or a scheme which depends for its existence upon the transient personal influence of a
few men. No doubt, a few men only know the full
details of the plans for the realization of this stupendous enterprise, but the whole nation is none
the less fired by their spirit and is working as a
unit in accordance with their directions. It is
literally true that Germany has "become Bis-
marckian. His heavy spirit has settled upon it.
It wears his scowl. It has adopted his brutality,
as it has his greatness. It has taken his criterion
of truth, which is Germanic; his indifference to
justice, which is savage; his conception of a state,
which is sublime." "This nation has forgotten
God in its exaltation of the Germanic race."
Bombastic as such phrases are, they do convey
some notion of the militant spirit which has

Mr. Hurd quotes the following sentences from the speech of the
Imperial Chancellor in the Reichstag on November 10, 1912: "For
months past we have been living, and we are living now, in an atmos-
phere of passion such as we have perhaps never before experienced
in Germany. At the root of this feeling is the determination of Germany to make its strength and capability prevail in the world."
See also the note at the end of this chapter.

roused that nation. When Li Hung Chang first learned from Bismarck the magnitude of these plans, he was skeptical. But before his brief stay in Germany was over, he wrote in his diary: "From all that I have seen, I am more than ever convinced that the Kaiser and Prince Bismarck meant what they said when they averred that the German Empire was destined to become a dominant factor in Europe."

The magnitude of the conception, the degree of success already attained, the probability of its complete realization, the grave dangers which it involves to other nations, are most clearly demonstrated by the alarm manifested by the latter. England's foremost soldier, Lord Roberts, has publicly declared that she has never been in all her history in a position of greater peril. The leader of the Opposition in the House of Commons as solemnly affirmed the truth of his statement. Ten years ago, he said, England had command of every sea; now she held control only of the North Sea. Ten years ago her fleet was so strong that she could have confidently expected to emerge victorious from a struggle of the magnitude of the Napoleonic wars; to-day there was no such probability. The ex-Premier of France, M. Clemenceau, said in public: "When I look towards the boundary of a territory which was French when

I was young, and when I see there the massing of lines of bayonets, I cannot dream of disarming." A crisis of the utmost gravity is thus facing Europe, and may at any moment result in a war whose consequences would be felt alike by the farmers in North Dakota, the operators in Lancashire cotton mills, and the savages in the heart of Africa. At the very least, it will overthrow political boundaries whose permanence has been thought assured; at the worst, it may involve the actual destruction of the prosperity and happiness of two or three of the largest countries in Europe and inflict untold misery upon the countless thousands dependent upon European rule in Africa and Asia.

The vital factor in the modern international situation is the aggression of Germany, her determination to expand her territories, to increase her wealth and power. Three centuries ago, Prussia was a tiny state whose many parts were separated from each other by the lands of her neighbors. Cut off from the sea on all sides, pushed hither by the oncoming Russian, dragged thither by the encroaching French, surrounded by tiny incompetent states, her rulers saw in aggression the only possible method of preserving the national life. To prevent her absorption by her neighbors, she must grow faster than they; she must rob

4

them instead of waiting for them to rob her. By war, she secured access to the Baltic; by war, she obtained the coveted Silesia; by war, she annexed much of Poland; by war, she spread her ægis over the whole of northern Germany. The humiliation of conquest she knew under Napoleon, and she has never forgotten nor ever will that no natural barriers stand between her and the invader. Poverty-stricken, still recovering from the ravages of the wars of the seventeenth and eighteenth centuries, menaced on all sides by powerful enemies, her only safety, Bismarck saw, lay in aggression, her only chance of victory depended upon striking the first blow. By this policy, she has built up one of the most powerful states in the world and one of the most populous and prosperous. But she has reached the boundaries of Germany; further expansion means the acquisition of what other nations now own.

The logic of facts, proving the necessity of expansion, is, to such Germans as General Bernhardi, unanswerable. The population has increased so rapidly that it is already difficult for efficient, well-trained men to secure any employment. Not only is the superficial area of the country suitable for cultivation practically exhausted, but intensive scientific agriculture is speedily limiting the possibilities of the employment of more hands on the same acres or the further increase of the produce. Industry has grown at a stupendous rate, and the output from German factories is enormously in excess of the needs of even the growing population. Her exports *per capita* are $24 a year, as against England's $40, and France's $25, and she has not their exclusive colonial markets. Unless some outlet can be found for the surplus population, and a new and extensive market discovered for this enormous surplus production, prosperity will be inevitably succeeded by bankruptcy. There will be more hands than there is work for, more mouths than there is food, and Germany must either get rid of the surplus mouths and hands or swell the surplus product by employing them at home, which cannot be done without entailing national ruin. Expansion is, therefore, the only alternative, for the German considers equivalent to ruin the reduction of the pressure of population by emigration,[1] and the avoidance of overproduction

[1] In 1881, nearly five per cent of the total population emigrated, and in the two succeeding years the number was scarcely smaller. Most of them came to the United States. German emigration at present is almost negligible. The name Pan-Germanism at first denoted a movement for the creation of a greater national unit out of these emigrants and the Germans at home. It aimed at maintaining the emigrants' devotion to the Fatherland by preserving their language and German habits, and at preventing their amalgamation, so far as possible, into the nation to which they had migrated. Its hope was eventually to draw them back to the Father-

by the proportionate reduction of output. For Germany to be thus forced to remain static in population and in wealth, while her neighbors continue to expand, England in her colonies, France in Morocco, Russia in Siberia and Turkestan, means that the date of her annihilation will be fixed by the rate of their growth. And such action on her part would compel her in fact to be an accessory to her own destruction, for her emigrants must strengthen her rivals both in the field and in the factory. To ask a German, therefore, whether the expansion of Germany is desirable, is merely to ask him whether he believes it desirable from any point of view for the German nation to survive.

Already the boundaries of Germany in Europe have been pushed to their furthest extent; more territory can be added only at the expense of other nations, either of her powerful rivals, France and Russia, or of her weaker neighbors, Belgium, Holland, Denmark, and Sweden. Nor would the accession of such territory solve the difficulty. All European nations are already experiencing to

land or to provide for them new homes under the German flag elsewhere. The methods employed were mainly educational, by means of German newspapers, active German departments in American universities, German societies, frequent visits to the great German "colonies" by German authors and professors. This movement, however, was soon merged into and dwarfed by the greater scheme now known as Pan-Germanism.

some degree the necessity of an outlet for their surplus population and manufactures. A war for expansion in Europe would be without purpose and could only be detrimental to all. Germany must find some territory suitable for development by her own people which is not already choked with men and women. She is seeking the counterpart of the fertile plains of western Canada, of the rich valleys of northern Africa, where her people may build a new Germany whose existence will strengthen her and not her rivals. But such a promised land, tenanted only by native races, is not to be found. Every really available spot is held by England, France, or Russia. Germany can, therefore, obtain colonies suitable for her purposes only at the expense of these last. This is what is meant by the oft-reiterated statements that England, France, and Russia are by their very existence inimical to Germany's welfare, that, if she is to escape ruin, she must fight them. The alternative to colonies is access to some new market for her products, so vast in extent and so unlimited in its capacity of continued absorption, that her surplusage of population can be provided with work at home, and thus prosperity and the increase of the national strength indefinitely insured. The total annual imports into her own colonies she knows to be well under

THE CAUSES OF GERMAN AGGRESSION

ten millions of dollars; the exports from England
to the English colonies alone she knows to total
several hundred millions of dollars.[1] Such a market she is determined to have, cost what it may.

One other fact marks England as the greatest
obstacle in the path of her legitimate growth.
The English Channel is the only available safe
passageway for her merchant fleets. The voyage
round the British Isles is long and during the
winter months positively dangerous even for
steamships. Natural conditions, therefore, by
compelling Germany to use the Channel, force
her to expose her commerce to the assaults of the
English fleet so long as the latter controls the
Channel. Even if she should acquire colonies and
a great market, she cannot really possess them
until she acquires a highroad to them safe from
the attacks of her enemies. Short of conquering
England and France, she can never free her commerce from actual danger; without a great fleet
in the North Sea, strong enough to terrify England
into inaction, she cannot even be assured of the
continuance of her present freedom of passage.[2]

[1] The leading customers of England in 1910 were in millions of
pounds: India, 45 millions; Germany, 37 millions; the United States,
31 millions; Australia, 27 millions; France, 22 millions; Canada, 19
millions. England's exports to these three colonies were 91 millions
and her exports to the three nations were 90 millions.

[2] The preface of the German Naval Bill of 1900 stated: "For the
protection of our oversea trade and our colonies, there is only one

9

Her fleet, therefore, seems to her merely the guarantee of her present position, and it will continue to be a guarantee only as long as its size makes it formidable. Merely to retain what she now has, Germany is condemned to increase her navy at any pace the English see fit to set. Something more will be absolutely essential if the dire consequences of an economic crisis are not to impoverish her and pave the way for her ultimate destruction at the hands of her hereditary enemies, France and Russia.

To secure a share of the world's trade in some fashion which will not expose her to the attacks of the English fleet, and which will create an empire less vulnerable in every way than she believes the British Empire to be, an overland route to the East must be found. The Germans consider perfectly feasible the construction of a great confederation of states including Germany, Austria, Hungary,

means: a strong fleet. Under the present circumstances, the only means for protecting Germany's oversea trade and colonies is: Germany must possess a fleet of such strength that a war, even with the strongest naval power, would involve such risks as to jeopardize the position of that power. For that purpose, it is not absolutely necessary that the German fleet be as strong as the fleet of the greatest naval power, for a great naval power will not generally be in a position to concentrate all its forces against Germany. But, even if the greatest naval power should succeed in meeting us with a fleet of superior strength, the defeat of a strong German fleet would so greatly weaken its own power, that, notwithstanding its victory, its own position on the seas would no longer be secure."

10

the Balkan States, and Turkey, which would control a great band of territory stretching southeast from the North Sea to the Persian Gulf. A railway from Constantinople to Baghdad would effectually tie the great trunk lines, leading from the Rhine and Danube valleys, to Constantinople and the Persian Gulf, and so establish a shorter route to India than that *via* Suez. Egypt, Syria, Arabia, Persia, India herself, the mother of nations, would fall into German hands and be held safe from conquest by this magnificent overland route to the East. Pan-Germanism is, therefore, in the first place, a defensive movement for self-preservation, for escaping the pressure of France and Russia, both bent on her destruction. It is, in the second place, an offensive movement directed against England, its object, the conquest of the English possessions in the Mediterranean and in Asia. She expects thus to obtain an outlet for her surplus population and manufactures and to create an empire as little vulnerable politically, economically, or strategically as any the world has yet seen.

In reply to the outcries from other nations, denouncing these plans as unprovoked aggression and lacking in morality, as a reversion to the forcible methods of bygone centuries whose brutalities the world long ago outgrew, the Germans

11

derisively point to the presence of the English in
India, of the French in Morocco, of the Russians
in Manchuria, of the United States in Panama.
They insist that their aims and methods are absolutely identical with those their detractors have
so long employed. Now that the latter's work is
complete and their own futures assured, they are
no doubt eager to establish "moral," "ethical,"
and "legal" precepts whose acceptance by other
nations would insure them the undisturbed possession of all they now hold. This, the Germans
admit, is but natural and not blameworthy; but
they ought not to expect other nations to sub-
scribe to such principles from motives of love or
admiration.[1] General Bernhardi, a man whose
undoubted attainments and learning compel the
respect of his enemies, and whose following in
Germany is large in numbers and influential in
character, declares openly that might is right, and
that right is decided by war. He scoffs at such
ideas of ethics and morality as his critics represent, and insinuates that, if war happened to

[1] "That any one should act in politics out of complaisance or from
a sentiment of justice, others may expect from us, but not we from
them. . . . Every government takes solely its own interests as the
standard of its actions, however it may drape them with deductions
of justice or sentiment. . . . My belief is that no one does anything
for us, unless he can at the same time serve his own interests." Bismarck, *Reflections and Reminiscences*, English translation, A. J.
Butler, New York and London, 1899, respectively, pp. 176, 173, 202.

promise other nations at this moment as many advantages as it does Germany, they would hold views similar to his upon that subject.

With him, the Germans as a whole refuse to admit the validity of any theoretical notions whose application would in any way restrict or interfere with Germany's "full share in the mastery of the world." Do they not see about them the splendidly tangible results of the investment [1] of the huge war indemnity paid by France to ransom her lands from the German army? Do they not know that the indemnity created modern Germany? As a prominent German manufacturer said to the writer two years ago, "Next time we will ask five times as much." In the face of the undeniable territorial gains, equal in amount to several times the area of Prussia and Brandenburg combined in 1640, in the face of that five billions of francs which they have invested and reinvested with such brilliant success for forty years, how can the Germans be expected to believe that the fruits of peace are greater than those

[1] The indemnity was nominally spent in defraying the cost of the war and in improving the army and fortifications. It was indirectly distributed to the nation and to individuals; for the army was the nation in arms, the debts were mostly owed to Germans, the labor and materials employed on the new works were German. However the transaction was recorded formally on the books of the state, the nation itself received the money either in wages or by the remission of taxes.

13

of war? Is not the very existence of Imperial
Germany due to war? Could it conceivably have
been created by anything else? Will anything less
preserve it? They deny the validity of any particular set of ethical notions of right and wrong
to decide issues vital to the continued existence
of the Germanic race. If such considerations are
to be dragged into the discussion, the notion of
the relativity of truth, the doctrine that moral and
ethical standards are not fixed but merely reflect
the stage of progress each particular age has
reached, the Darwinian doctrine of the survival
of the fittest, all seem to them infinitely more
satisfactory theoretical grounds for action than
what Bismarck sneeringly called "the English
phrases about humanity."

The most significant question now before the
Anglo-Saxon race, therefore, is the truth or falsity of those notions of strategical geography, of
military and naval organization, of finance and
commerce upon which these vast schemes are
based. If the factors, on which the Germans rely,
are what they think they are, the domination of
the world by Germany and her allies can be only
a question of time. If they are not valid, the
world will certainly develop along different lines.
So widely do the economic and political interests
ramify, so completely are all sections of the globe

influenced by them, that nothing can happen, from this moment until the final decision of the issue, which will not vitally affect it or be vitally affected by it. The Boer War, Morocco, the strangling of Persia, the war in Tripoli, the Balkan crisis are only incidents in this gigantic struggle in which the very pawns are kingdoms and the control of the entire globe the stake. Indeed, the forces at the disposal of the combatants are so comprehensive that navies and armies might almost be called incidental factors, which it may or may not be necessary to employ, and which might not indeed be decisive for victory or defeat.

Naturally, even to sketch the history of the world in its relation to the modern crisis, even to enumerate the multifold phases, political, constitutional, economic, military, which it necessarily displays, is an impossibility in anything briefer than a series of volumes. An attempt to describe merely the features and factors essential to a comprehension of the most significant phases of Pan-Germanism alone will require the omission of much that is important and will make impossible any account at all of the narrative of recent history. What has happened, what is happening, is of infinitely less consequence than the scope and character of the German plans. The most vital fact for the Anglo-Saxon race to grasp at present is the German view of European history, of European life and ideals, their estimation of the comparative strength of political, economic, and ethical forces. From a grasp of these points, and from it alone, can we hope to understand the apparently inexplicable and inconsistent ideas upon which has been based the most audacious attempt yet made consciously to direct through a long term of years the evolution of a nation and the fate of the world.[1] The following chapters, therefore, will attempt to describe Europe and Germany, as the Germans see them, as the necessary prelude to a brief statement of the progress Germany has made toward a realization of her scheme and a description of the attempts of her "victims" to frustrate it. Then, there will

[1] The extent to which the German nation as a whole is conscious of the existence of Pan-Germanism is not demonstrable. There can be no doubt that the Government has consistently attempted to shape public opinion in favor of it. Bismarck's notion of public opinion is enlightening. He said to Crispi: "Public opinion is but a great river formed by a quantity of small streams, one of which is the Government stream. If the Government would but swell its waters sufficiently, it would have a determinative influence upon the great public current. If, on the contrary, the Government wants to measure the strength of all the other streams, which, separately, are less powerful than its own, it must be overwhelmed by the union of their forces. A Government acting thus would be guilty of unpardonable neglect of precautions." Crispi, *Memoirs*, II, 163, London, 1912.

In the *Fortnightly Review*, XCI, New Series, 785, Archibald Hurd states: "A section of powerful politicians and vested interests, with the support of the Emperor and the Marine Amt, under Grand-Admiral von Tirpitz, have obtained control of the Government and the most influential newspapers, and dominate German policy."

be an opportunity to weigh the scheme in the balance, to point out its elements of strength and weakness, and thus to arrive at some approximation of the probability of its success or failure.

NOTE

The following testimony was given under oath in a court of law by the editor of the *Rheinisch-Westfälische Zeitung* in a political libel suit instituted by him against the editor of the *Grenzboten*. It was printed only [so far as can be learned] by the *Rheinisch-Westfälische Zeitung* and the *Tägliche Rundschau*, but was not denied by the gentlemen named in it, and seems to have been suppressed so far as was possible. The following translation is taken from a semi-official article in the *Fortnightly Review*, xci, New Series, 462. Whether or not the words credited to the important personages quoted were ever used, they express sentiments which are widely believed to represent their views. After all, it is not so much the truth itself, but what intelligent and sincere men believe to be the truth, which influences the trend of human events.

"Mr. Class, the President of the Pan-Germanic League, is prepared *to state upon oath before this court* [1] that the Secretary of State for Foreign Affairs, Herr von Kiderlen Wächter, writing to him from Kissingen, requested Mr. Class to meet him at the Hotel Pfälzer Hof in Mannheim. During the interview, which occupied several hours, Herr von Kiderlen Wächter stated: 'The Pan-Germanic demand for the possession of Morocco is absolutely justified. You can absolutely

[1] The italics are not in the original.

rely upon it that the Government will stick to Morocco. Monsieur Cambon is wriggling before me like a worm. The German Government is in a splendid position. You can rely upon me and you will be very pleased with our Morocco policy. *I am as good a Pan-German as you are.*[1] On the 1st of July, Mr. Class called at the German Foreign Office, and, failing to find Herr von Kiderlen Wächter, was received by Herr Zimmermann, the Under-Secretary. Mr. Zimmermann told him: 'You come at an historic hour. To-day the Panther appears before Agadir and at this moment (12 o'clock mid-day) the Foreign Cabinets are being informed of its mission. The German Government has sent two *agents provocateurs* to Agadir and these have done their duty very well. German firms have been induced to make complaints and to call upon the Government in Berlin for protection. It is the Government's intention to seize the district and it will not give it up again. The German people require absolutely a settlement colony. Please prevent, wherever in the Press you have influence, the raising of claims for compensation elsewhere. Possibly France will offer us the Congo. However, the German does not want compensation elsewhere, but a part of Morocco.'"

[1] The italics are not in the original.

CHAPTER II

THE MYTH OF ENGLISH PREPONDERANCE IN EUROPE

ENGLAND, with all her bluster and show," said Bismarck to Li Hung Chang, "has a hundred weak points, and she knows that a conflict with a power nearly her equal will mean her undoing." A vital part of the German scheme for the control of the world depends upon the belief that power is not absolute, but comparative. Not alone Germany's strength, but her rivals' weakness, will be significant factors for victory or defeat. To Germans it is an error to suppose that England is decadent. The fundamental misconception is to suppose that England ever was strong. She has been strong by reason of others' weakness, by the use of others' resources, by the spoils of conquest. She has not less cohesion than before, not fewer vital interests in common with her dependencies. The British Empire has never possessed cohesion; never has had a common, vital economic, or geographical interest; has always been a sham, a figment of the imagination, a glittering generality whose unreality has remained concealed only by reason of the inability of other nations to perceive it.[1]

England's naval power has been the result of accident, not of genius, think the Germans, and has rested chiefly upon the accidents of geography and geology. The formation of the British Isles, the meeting of strong oceanic currents to the north of them, made the narrow passageway between England and Europe the most important single bit of water in the world. The commerce of northern Europe was forced to pass through the Channel because it could not safely go round. The navigation of this safer passage was made exceedingly difficult for wooden sailing ships by the peculiar formation of the shores and by the treacherous tides, winds, and currents. Chance had, moreover, placed most of the natural harbors on the English side. There was, indeed, between Brest and Hamburg but one spot on the continental side which might serve as a base of operations for a great fleet, the district now known as the Neth-

[1] The author begs his readers to bear carefully in mind that he is attempting in the following chapters to expound the German view of the situation rather than what he believes to be the truth. Naturally, a view of the international situation, upon which a great nation of intelligent people is willing to base a policy on whose success may depend their national future, will contain many factors whose truth is not to be denied by any impartial student. The general conclusions, derived from considering these obviously true facts, may, however, be vulnerable.

erlands. The constant use of the Channel necessarily involved, therefore, the use of English harbors as a refuge from storms. Nor were the difficulties of navigation limited to the passage of ships
through the Channel. To sail across that narrow
way, especially with a fleet, was literally an almost
impossible feat except from one or two points on
the European shore, the more favorable of which
was the Netherlands. The natural barriers to
invasion thus furnished by the Channel so limited
the possibilities of assault that its defense became
comparatively simple. Invasion after invasion,
decade after decade, was defeated because the
unfavorable weather, continuing for weeks at a
time, made it impossible for the enemy to leave
Europe. These natural barriers are gone forever,
destroyed by the steamship, which is not limited
in the time of its departure nor in its course by
winds and waves.[1] Never again can an English

[1] The German Navy League issued in 1912 a book entitled,
Deutschland Sei Wach, in which this statement was made prominent:
"The maintenance of Great Britain's naval supremacy which has
been kept unimpaired during the last century, has, through the relative strength of the German fleet, become impossible in the future.
That is the great historic process which we are seeing. It is no more
to be imagined that England can destroy the German fleet without
seriously compromising her own supremacy." At the end of the volume in the very largest of type stands the following: "Germany
must be strong on land, so strong that she can vanquish every opponent, but she must also be so strong at sea that she need not fear any
opponent, because the risk of a naval war would be so great that it
would appear too great even to the strongest naval Power."

fleet adopt Nelson's tactics of allowing the weather to guard the Channel while he crushed the enemy elsewhere. Napoleon, waiting at Boulogne, once truly said that seven hours of darkness and a fair wind would change the fate of the world. In the next war the invader will not need to pray for either.

The Germans also correctly appreciate the fact that the English control of the Baltic — the only considerable source of naval stores from which wooden fleets might be built or maintained — was a vital factor in their naval supremacy. Not only did they possess a superior fleet; they possessed the chief supply of materials from which rival fleets could be built. Trafalgar gave England supremacy on the sea, not so much because she won the battle, as because her control of the sea prevented Napoleon from obtaining the materials out of which alone he might rebuild his shattered fleet. This monopoly is gone forever. Ships are now built of a material of which no nation has a monopoly, and of which England does not even control one of the chief sources of supply.

The peculiar strategical geography of northern Europe the Germans also hold responsible for England's power. The land on either side of the mouth of the Rhine is the key to northern Europe.

Belgium controls the shortest route to Paris; Holland is the only point of departure from which an invasion of England is likely to be successful; both countries hold between them the door of the Rhine valley, the gateway to the heart of Germany. Their possession by any one of the three nations nearest them would give her immediately a most deadly offensive weapon against the other two. To possess them has been the dream of all; to secure them half the wars in European history have been fought. Those two tiny states are now independent because England, France, and Germany cannot permit each other to control them. To the east lies the gateway between France and Germany, Alsace-Lorraine, through whose fair fields pass the roads to Cologne and Berlin, to Frankfort, Leipzig, and Dresden, to Basel, Switzerland, and Italy, to the Danube valley and Vienna. Its possession permits France to enter the heart of Germany; its possession puts Germany at the very doors of France; it is a potent weapon of offense or defense and enables its holder to begin a war with tremendous advantages. For its possession, France and Germany have struggled for fifteen hundred years. The existence of these strategic points has made England important. If France assailed the Rhine from Lorraine, Germany would ally with England, who could assail

Paris from the north through Belgium. If Germany threatened France from the east, the English might be induced to invade Germany from the Netherlands. Should either country obtain the coöperation of England against the other, the most disastrous results were probable. These conditions made England a factor in politics during the Middle Ages, out of all proportion to her actual strength as compared with France or Germany. She was in a position to deliver a deadly flank attack on either; the Channel effectually prevented retaliation; she could have consummated the dynastic ambitions of either; she preferred to thwart the aims of both. When the Netherlands fell into Spanish hands in the sixteenth century and the power of the Hapsburgs threatened to absorb all Europe, the coöperation of the islanders, who controlled the stormy Channel and who could so easily invade the Netherlands, was seen by every one to be the controlling factor in a complex situation. Their assistance would almost certainly decide the war in favor of France or Spain. Not England's strength, but the fact that her position made her valuable to stronger nations, gave her a voice in the days of Henry VIII and Elizabeth. Not her strength, but the evenness of the balance of power in Europe, the rivalry of Bourbon and Hapsburg, their fear of each other, gave her the casting vote.[1]

Until the nineteenth century, France was the only strong, organic nation on the continent of Europe: Spain, Italy, and Germany were geographical expressions, whose weakness and fear of France forced them to call on England for aid. No doubt immense significance ought to be attached to England's own condition during these same centuries. She attained in the days of William the Norman, in the eleventh century, a territorial unity which Spain did not attain until the fifteenth century, France until the sixteenth century, Germany and Italy until the nineteenth century. Her strong centralized monarchy, certainly the most powerful feudal government in Europe, the strong Tudor monarchy in later years were able to throw into the European balance the whole force of a territorial and economic unit. England, united and ruled by a single king, easily able to suppress local uprisings, was

[1] "England has always caused one Power to destroy another Power. Herein lies England's profit." "The great Wars of Religion in Germany made it possible for England to become a sea power. During the time when Germany was torn and enfeebled, England could destroy the Hanseatic League. Prussia's Seven Years' War enabled England to oust the old Colonial Powers and to seize French Canada. . . . The final conquest of the New World succeeded only because Frederick the Great held down France in Europe." *England's Weltherrschaft und die Deutsche Luxusflotte, von Lookout.* Berlin, February, 1912. Fourteen editions were sold in a few weeks.

actually stronger than a vastly more populous
and wealthy state, like France, Germany, or
Spain, whose international strength was limited
to such force as could be exerted by that one of her
princes who had been able to secure the ascendency for the time being, and who was invariably
hard pressed at home by ambitious rivals scarcely
less powerful than he. The strategical position
of the continental nations laid them open to invasion from so many quarters that they must be
continually withholding from their offensive army
in one place enough men to insure safety in others.
Not so England, whom the Channel enabled to
concentrate her forces at one point without fear
of invasion elsewhere. England fought with her
whole strength those who had not yet finished
fighting among themselves. The number of years
during which England has been the scene of actual
warfare are astonishingly few. Since the days of
Henry VIII, there has been domestic peace except
for the civil wars of the seventeenth century.
Such a record no other nation can show. Nor were
the wars which did take place on English soil
as disastrous or destructive as the wars on the
Continent. When the Continent was almost laid
waste, England could husband or utilize her full
economic strength at will. Not alone, therefore,
because of her position and the rivalries of others

has England played the controlling part in international affairs. Compared to any individual nation, her strength has been great.

The growth during the nineteenth century of Prussia, Austria, and Italy has given England as rivals, in place of the old decentralized, inefficient, quarreling federations of tiny states, strong centralized governments, larger than she in area, with more numerous populations, with greater resources. She has lost her old position, despite the fact that she was never more prosperous or better governed than she is at present, because of the proportionately more rapid development of her rivals. Nor can she longer claim a more efficient use of her resources than they. For a strong king, has been substituted a ministry; for the rapidity, vigor, and secrecy of the king's unhampered discretion, has been substituted the less rapid and efficient direction of a many-headed executive whose actions are hampered and hindered by the House of Commons. However admirable the results of parliamentary government have been for the individual Englishman, it can scarcely be denied that the new democratic government is comparatively less efficient than the old centralized monarchy, and that, from the international point of view, England has lost immensely in offensive strength.

27

In the Government, too, exist the gravest dissensions. The assumption has always been that there would be a clear majority in the House of Commons in favor of one of two policies; that the Ministry would represent this majority, and from its unity and strength would derive support for the exercise of the discretionary authority necessary for all emergencies. Yet, for twenty years, the English parties in the House of Commons have both remained almost constant in size, and the decision has usually rested with the Irish and labor members, who have entertained views highly inconsistent with policy as the great majority of the English people have conceived it. And these two parties, thus fortuitously placed in so commanding a position, have more than once given clear expression to their determination to use the exigencies of the occasion to extort from the reluctant English the consent necessary for the attainment of their own aims. In fact, it is not Ireland but England that needs home rule. The constitutional development of the nineteenth century has, for the time being, made difficult the efficient use of English resources. Lord Esher recently gave public expression to the opinion that the difficulty of coördinating the offensive and defensive forces of the nation made impracticable the adoption by the military authorities in

England "of a plan, Napoleonic in scope and design, and resting upon a centralized basis."

During these same decades, precisely the opposite type of development has taken place in Europe. The decentralized administration, which so long rendered impotent the great resources of Germany, Austria, and Italy in men and money, was replaced in each country by a centralized monarchy whose efficiency made the prompt utilization of every resource a certainty. Where in England the direction of policy passed from the hands of a few into the hands of many, in Germany, Austria, and Italy it passed, from the hands of many princes, with various antagonistic aims, into the hands of a few men whose ideas were essentially the same. The fact that such development could not be foreseen does not alter its significance. England no longer possesses as much strength as she used to have; relatively to her rivals, she has suffered even more seriously, for while she has gone backward, they have gone forward. Compared to what she used to be, she is actually administratively weaker; compared with her rivals, she is relatively not twice but four times less strong than she used to be.

Her "control of the sea" has also been vitally changed by the development of Europe during the last three centuries. The offensive power of the

English fleet naturally must depend upon the possibility of injuring the enemy either by the destruction of his warships or by the cutting of lines of communication vital to his commerce. In the old days, the absence of good roads compelled the transportation of bulky goods by water, and the extent of the facilities for water communication was the measure of the size of that country's trade. In northern Europe, merchandise necessarily traveled down a series of parallel rivers into the English Channel, the North Sea, and the Baltic, through which it proceeded to its destination. Goods could be shipped from Cologne to Hamburg only through the Channel and the North Sea. Most of the internal trade between different parts of Germany or France was thus exposed in transit to the operations of the English fleet. All commerce by sea between northern Europe and the Mediterranean or the East was forced to go through the English Channel, exposed to the English fleet and the Channel weather.[1] But the

[1] "On every one of the world's trade routes, like an ancient robber knight in full armor, lance in hand, stands England. All nations must run the gauntlet of England. . . . The domination of the world on the sea enables the supreme naval Power to inflict the most terrible crises upon other nations. Every nation must combat this predominance for the sake of its future. . . . All nations have become tributary to the city of London, some more, some less. Germany would find existence at England's sufferance unbearable." *England's Weltherrschaft und die Deutsche Luxusflotte.*

coming of the railway in the nineteenth century destroyed for all time this phase of England's sea power. The internal trade of Germany, and, indeed, much of her international trade, goes overland by rail and is thus entirely freed from the menace of English assault. Even with the Far East, trade is possible by rail, and the coming decade will undoubtedly see a further development of transcontinental trunk lines. The importance, therefore, of the Channel as the chief means of intercommunication in northern Europe has disappeared, and with it has gone England's control of the trade of northern Europe.

Further, England's prosperity in the eighteenth and nineteenth centuries was due in no small degree to her control of the chief or only supplies of sugar, tobacco, tea, coffee, cotton goods, and all those varied products supplied by the East and West Indies. For those the Continent depended upon her, as Napoleon discovered when the imposition of the Continental System excluded English goods from the European market. The men actually seemed to resent far more the loss of their tobacco, and the women the deprivation of their tea, than they had the destruction of the political units to which they had formerly owed allegiance. The Continental System failed to bankrupt England because Europe absolutely refused to do without English goods. Another trade monopoly, far more fundamental, was due to England's industrial revolution of the eighteenth century. The smelting of iron with coal, the blast furnace, the steam hammer revolutionized the working of metals; the new spinning and weaving machinery, the stationary steam engine and the factory revolutionized all industry; the breeding of cattle, the use of the turnip, of manure, and of selected seeds revolutionized agriculture. Such significant economic changes had not been seen since man began to record his own doings. For more than a generation, England enjoyed the exclusive monopoly of these processes and the consequent benefits. English goods commanded higher prices because they were more uniform; English profits were again larger than European to the extent that machinery was cheaper than the old hand processes. England was, therefore, economically doubly more powerful than any other nation in Europe, because she alone controlled the supply of commodities which Europe insisted upon having, and because she alone possessed the secret of the improved processes. But her advantage in these respects has disappeared. Sugar cane from Louisiana and Hawaii, American cotton, Brazilian coffee, and the complete utilization by her chief rivals of all modern inventions has robbed her of the unique economic position she held in 1815.

In fact, to the German, England's economic strength has been changed into fatal economic weakness. She no longer produces sufficient food to supply her population for a month; her supplies of coal and wood are diminishing at a rate which causes serious reflection; the raw material needed to supply her looms and factories she does not produce; the raw material to build or maintain a fleet she cannot produce.[1] The area of land under cultivation has steadily diminished. Population on the soil is decreasing at a more rapid rate and is drifting into the cities, where it further complicates the serious economic and administrative problems which worry her rulers. Every family moved from the land into the factory means so many less individuals who supply themselves with the necessities of life, so many more dependent upon the perfect operation of a complicated economic machinery for feeding them. Suppose now that the German fleet could secure control of the Channel for a brief time only, would not England

[1] "Were it possible to cut off Great Britain's supply of food, in less than six weeks the inhabitants would die of starvation. Britons are fully aware of the danger, and all, from the noble lord to the laborer, are convinced that it is the most important duty of the State to keep open and secure the broad highway of the ocean." *Die Flotte als notwendige Ergänzung unserer nationalen Wehrmacht*, by A. Schröder, a book written for the German secondary schools.

be starved into submission, would not her looms soon stop from the lack of material to feed them, would not her whole artisan class be thrown out of work, would not she be bankrupted as a nation in the most fundamental fashion by the simple loss of the control of the sea? Once the English fleet were beaten, could she ever obtain material with which to rebuild it, as long as the German fleet existed? Disaster on the sea would infallibly mean for England economic destruction at the hands of elemental foes far more potent than armies. And it would be irretrievable! Each decade, moreover, brings it nearer and nearer, by diminishing the number of mouths that feed themselves and increasing the number to be fed by the fleet; nearly every year shortens the length of time which the Germans must control the Channel in order literally to destroy England by means of the economic weapons which control of the Channel would enable them to wield.

Furthermore, the Germans believe that so many years of peace, otherwise so fruitful of advantages, have produced the most serious results upon the temper of the people. They are no longer warlike. They are unwilling to bear the burdens of taxation which the preparation for a great war renders inevitable. The spreading among them of humanitarian notions has actually

34

deprived them of morale, rendered them supine,
and apt material for conquest.[1] Not only has England no army worth considering, but she has not
the human stuff out of which great armies are
made, for her people are not as a whole willing
to coöperate in the creation of the only sort of
army of any avail in modern warfare. In fact, the
German notion of England is not so seriously
exaggerated by such words as these: "Look at
England — fat and fifty, overfed, short of breath,
thickening in girth, deepening in brain. . . . England, entering upon her inevitable period of physical decadence, boasting of conquests, like a middle-
aged man with rheum in his eye, the clog of senility
under his waistcoat, stiffness in his joints, and the
red lights of apoplexy bright upon his throat —
who throws out his chest among his sons and
pants that he is 'better than ever, e'gad!' England, sensuous in the home, crowding her homes
like a squirrel's nest in the frosts; an animated
stomach, already cultivating and condimenting
her fitful but necessary appetites; wise and crafty
in the world, but purblind to her own perversions

[1] "During many decades German university professors, school-
masters, and publicists have taught the doctrine that Englishmen
were too selfish and too cowardly to defend their country, and that
England, like Carthage, was bound to fall through the lack of patriotism among the people and their reliance upon hired soldiers."
Fortnightly Review, xci, New Series, 456.

and lying in the rot of them — England, who will not put away boyish things and look to God. . . . She is draining India as Rome drained Gaul, as Spain drained Mexico, and accelerating the bestiality that spells ruin — with the spoils."

CHAPTER III

TO the German, the grandeur and splendor of Imperial England which has so long been impressed upon the world is nothing but bluster and show, masking congenital weakness of the most serious description. Some have not scrupled to say that Imperial England is nothing but a trading monopoly, a chain of forts, a great fleet, and a monumental impudence. That the English won their empire by force of arms, the Germans deny. It is hardly likely that a few thousand men, even headed by a beardless clerk who turned out to be a genius, could conquer by strength or craft the teeming millions of Hindus. Miracles are no longer common, and such miracles as fill the annals of the history of the building of the English Empire, as told by Englishmen, have never happened. The Empire is not a reality; it is a sham.

The Germans quote with satisfaction such statements regarding the position of the English in India as Lord Curzon's remark that the English are only a bit of froth upon an unfathomable ocean. That, they deem to be no mere rhetorical flourish, as the English believe it to be, but the bare statement of the literal truth regarding the strength of the English hold on India. Really, the English never have conquered India. The Hindus, with the assistance of the English, conquered each other. Had it not been for the existence in India of many races, many languages, many religions, and those multitudinous jealousies and antipathies which grew out of them and filled the annals of that unhappy country with a record of discord and treachery, the English would not even be at this moment the froth tossing on that restless sea. They continue to rule by reason of those same factors which lay at the bottom of their so-called conquest and which make unity of the native races impossible. The Germans, nevertheless, do not fail to appraise at its true value the skill and tact which they have displayed in utilizing these factors. Knowing that physical force of their own could never maintain their authority or impose upon the really powerful native rulers regulations not to their liking, they have taken the greatest care to do what the Hindus would permit, rather than what they themselves felt to be desirable. A single native state — the only alternative to united rule by the English — has always been impossible of realization because of the variety of races forced by the exigencies of the past to dwell together in the great plains of the Himalayas. In fact, the English have succeeded to that shadowy authority known in the olden time as the Sovereignty of the Emperor, and have correctly interpreted it to confer upon them the right of direction, of suggestion, of assistance, not of control. Undoubtedly they have helped the Hindu rulers by the businesslike administration of their estates; by showing them better methods of collecting the taxes, of utilizing their revenues, of administering justice. The condition of the peasants has been vastly improved, and has not, as the rajahs feared, reduced their authority or diminished the loyalty of their subjects. But could not Germans also do as much? Do the English give the Hindu anything which the Germans could not give as well? Have the English ever earned the enduring gratitude of the Hindu?

The English power in India has to no small degree depended, the Germans think, upon that obvious fact that they have had no competitors for the exercise of their overlordship in India since the middle of the eighteenth century. Their supremacy on the sea, which rested upon their control of the Channel, upon their wonderful seamanship, upon their practical monopoly of the naval stores in the Baltic, enabled them to keep far from

India any possible European rival. The whole of the Atlantic and Indian Oceans lay between India and any nation who wished to challenge England's rights there. Furthermore, there was no overland route to India sufficiently practical for military purposes, nor was there in Europe any nation except France strong enough and sufficiently well organized to undertake so colossal a feat as the invasion of India. In fact, the English have remained in India, as they say, supreme for a century and a half, solely because they have prevented the natives from uniting against them, and have yet to defend themselves from a determined assault from without. Now that the old supremacy on the sea is vitally altered in character, that the strategical position of the Channel and the monopoly of the naval stores have disappeared, that the Baghdad Railroad is nearly finished, that a Russian railroad is within striking distance of Herat, the isolation of India has practically vanished. A very little force from without, a little discord within, and the waves will swallow up that bit of froth.

In the Mediterranean the English Empire has rested upon similar forces. The native races were at odds with themselves and with each other; the other Mediterranean powers were weak or hopelessly divided, and were unable to create in the

Mediterranean a fleet to cope with England without first bringing their materials through the Channel which she controlled. These conditions have so vitally changed that the rule of the English in Egypt can now, say the Germans, scarcely be considered as more than a transient phase in the long line of Egyptian administrative failures. For some decades England practically controlled Greece, Turkey, and the Balkans, exercising a very intangible and shadowy suzerainty exceedingly difficult to define, without effective powers for controlling or directing, to say nothing of utilizing, the resources of those countries. England possessed whatever degree of authority she had, not for administrative reasons of significance or value to the countries themselves, but to keep other nations at a distance. Turkey was not so much to obey England's behests as to frustrate Russia's designs. The same factors which have elsewhere sapped the peculiar structure of the English Empire have here also performed deadly work. There are now other strong powers possessed of fleets in the Mediterranean, able to equip and maintain them from their own resources, and possessed of the will to contest the control of the Mediterranean with her.

The long list of strategic points in England's hands does not frighten the Germans. It is little to them that England holds the Mediterranean, the Red Sea, the Indian Ocean, and controls the passageway between the Indian Ocean and the Yellow Sea, Magellan Strait, the Cape of Good Hope, and the most advantageous coaling-stations on all these routes. Such a chain of forts and islands would be useful as the bases for the action of a fleet of the old type, operating against similar fleets in a war between England, as she was, against her enemies, as they were. To protect so long a chain, England must keep a "masking fleet" at each threatened point. The work of science in creating steel ships, moved by steam, has compelled England to concentrate her fleet in the North Sea, has built up powerful rivals whose operations are not restricted by the considerations of a century ago, and has forced her to leave undefended all but a few points. It is doubtful whether England can be again defended at Trafalgar, or India saved at Aboukir. Every chain is as strong as its weakest link, and the chain of English strategical positions seems to the Germans certain to yield to an attack in force delivered at any point.

There can, furthermore, be no doubt that in all parts of the English Empire the old condition upon which England's rule of the native races depended, the supineness and inefficiency of native administration, has given way before the ambitions, of at least the educated natives, for autonomy. The democratic impulse which has so strongly manifested itself in Europe has also appeared in the Mediterranean and in the East. Already the Egyptian, the Persian, and the Hindu are dreaming of a new land from which foreigners shall be excluded, of a splendid nation composed solely of natives administering their own country in their own interests, paying tribute to no one, independent of all. English rule is hardly likely, the Germans think, to be permanent, even if the forces at present at work are allowed to develop in their normal way. The chief thing, in fact, which helped the English was the natives' lack of initiative and desire to rule themselves. The English undertook the burden of government which the native did not want. Now that the native is aroused by a sense of the possibilities of self-government, and has come to believe himself capable of securing for himself the sort of administration the English have given him, he is hardly likely to acquiesce much longer in English rule. Would it not now be easy for a nation to secure from all England's subjects the exclusive right to trade with them in exchange for a little assistance in putting the government of their own country into their own hands, and for promises

to protect them in future from outside interference ?

While not the most apparent, the most vital
weakness of the Empire lies in its own size. England in one way or another controls to some extent territory in every quarter of the globe. There
is scarcely a nation at whose doors there does
not lie some valuable English dependency which
she would be glad to have. The extent of the
booty is the measure of England's enemies. There
is too much to be divided, should she fall, for her
to survive long, assert the Germans. The cupidity
of too many nations is already aroused to make
possible any adequate assistance in propping up
the frail and worthless fabric. Where literally the
whole world has something to gain which England
alone will lose, is it not likely that one defeat in
any part of the world would so shake English prestige and so instantly reveal the rottenness of her
imperial fabric as to cause a rush for the plunder
similar to that which marked the downfall of the
Napoleonic Empire in 1814?

The bond between England and her self-governing colonies is even weaker, say the Germans, and
has infinitely fewer factors of fundamental importance to keep it in existence. Canada is separated
from England by the width of the Atlantic; South
Africa by the whole length of the Atlantic, a

distance nearly equal to the length of the globe; Australia is more than twelve thousand miles from Liverpool; and these enormous distances effectively prevent these colonies from possessing an economic interest in common with the mother country. Nor is it probable that any strong interest could possibly be created. Despite the progress of steam navigation, the voyage to them is still so long as to prevent any real coöperation in time of peace, or any effective assistance in time of war. There is no natural geographical basis for the British Empire. Such enormous tracts of land, so thinly populated, so far distant from each other, have nothing but the accident of their discovery and settlement by men of the same race to give them even that appearance of unity and common interest that they do possess. Unquestionably, the concentration of the English fleet in the North Sea and in the Mediterranean has deprived her colonies of the only thing they could have been expected to value. While it is not likely that any of them will require the services of a fleet to protect them from any enemies who would normally attack them, England can certainly no longer promise them such protection. They possess no privilege in England, or as a result of their connection with England, which the Germans themselves do not have. No trading privileges in

England, or with England, are theirs. If they were to declare their complete independence to-morrow, nothing would be changed. Indeed, it is literally true, and the English themselves admit it; that the Empire has been held together in name during the last century by resolutely sacrificing its reality.

Why should the colonies fight for the maintenance of an empire whose existence is not of benefit to them and whose destruction could not injure them? How could they furnish England any effective assistance in a war fought in the North Sea, the Mediterranean, or the Near East? Even should they send troops or supplies so far, their population is not large enough nor their resources sufficient, think the Germans, and above all their military organization is not enough perfected, to make such support decisive for victory. Besides, Canada would expose herself to assault from the United States, a danger which the Germans seem to think sufficiently real to detain the Canadian regiments at home; Australia would be exposed to the Japanese, of whom the Germans think they stand in daily fear; in Africa, the English confederation is exposed to the much more real danger of an attack from German East or West Africa, and besides is sufficiently imperiled by the disparity in numbers between the whites and the natives.

46

THE FATAL WEAKNESS OF ENGLAND

Indeed, it is conceivable that in Africa the English colonies would be in such danger from the outbreak of a war with Germany that they would be compelled in self-defense to sever their connection with the Empire. The loyalty of the colonies as a whole has been verbal, personal, a matter of sentiment, with which interests have never been allowed to clash. That it will stand the strain of real sacrifice, the Germans believe highly improbable.

The boasted millions of population, the countless acres of territory, the stupendous wealth of the British Empire are real — but they are not England's. They belong to peoples more widely sundered in race, language, and interests than are the English and the Germans. Indeed, there are many vital facts common to the latter which the English colonies utterly lack, and which they can never possess. The English Empire has never been a reality, nor ever will be. Its weakness merely needs to be made apparent.

CHAPTER IV

ENGLAND, Germany hates, disdains, and despises. For France and Russia she possesses a wholesome respect mingled with fear, but not with love. France, she considers a strong man who has run his race and is now beginning to reach senility; Russia, she looks upon as an uncouth stripling not yet conscious of his strength, not yet skillful enough to use the strength of which he is conscious, and not yet intelligent enough to avoid being easily deceived. There are, perhaps, no more characteristic pages in Bismarck's memoirs than those in which he discusses the comparative ease of deceiving the English, French, and Russians.

The strategic position of Germany renders her singularly open to attack from France and Russia. The three nations occupy the vast plain sloping to the Atlantic Ocean and the Baltic from the crests of the Jura and the Alps, a great plain with no natural barriers separating, one from another, the different peoples who occupy it. There is no

48

special reason for placing the German boundary at one spot rather than another; France has invariably claimed the Rhine as her natural boundary; Russia looks upon the whole Baltic as her especial property of which she is most unfairly deprived. The ambitions of both nations are of vital import to Germany, for France can obtain her natural boundary, or Russia, in Peter the Great's expressive words, can open her windows only at Germany's expense. Certainly, there can be little doubt that the expansion of either France or Russia means economic and political death for Germany by depriving a large section of her territory of the control of the natural highways. There are, furthermore, no mountains, no deep rivers demarking the present lines between her and her neighbors. Her only fortifications are the regiments of the German army. At the same time, if Germany is open to attack, the door also stands open for her to assault her enemies. No natural barriers prevent her from annexing land either along the Rhine or in Poland. Her expansion in Europe, therefore, is possible, but it means, inevitably, that she must take from her two powerful neighbors or absorb the smaller nations, Belgium, Holland, and Denmark, whose existence her rivals regard as necessary to their own safety.

Germany, fully realizing the seriousness of the

situation, at the same time confidently expects to turn it to her own advantage. It is perfectly true that she stands between France and Russia; but the central position, deadly to a weak nation, will afford so strong a nation as she an enviable opportunity for the offense. Her armies can support each other without severing their communications, can deliver an attack in force on either side with equal facility, while the most that her rivals can hope to do is to deliver a simultaneous attack from two sides. Actual coöperation between them, the massing of forces at the same time, at the same spot, is so difficult as to be practically impossible.

Again, she already holds the most important ports on the Baltic, and by the cutting of the Kiel Canal through the Danish peninsula has robbed Denmark of much of her strategic importance and has united the Baltic with the Atlantic Ocean by a passageway which she exclusively controls. Could she now secure possession of Denmark, she would not only possess freedom of passage for herself, but she could close the Baltic to Russia and England. She already holds Alsace-Lorraine, and stands on the very borders of France with many strategic posts of the utmost importance in her hands. On the northwest she impinges upon the French frontier at many points so near Paris that she is confident of an entry into the French capital a few days after the beginning of the campaign. The Russian fleet in the Baltic is not sufficiently powerful, she thinks, to be dangerous. The French fleet is not enough of a factor in the Atlantic to frighten her. She fears their armies, not their fleets. She does not underestimate the strength of their position, the size of their population, their wealth, or their patriotism. She does not believe them sufficiently well organized to utilize to the full their resources, and she is confident that nothing short of a complete utilization of every resource can make them really dangerous to her.

The most vital weakness in France, say the Germans, is the Republic. French administration, by the admission of French publicists themselves, is inefficient, failing to secure the best men for office, failing to keep competent men in office, failing to keep out of vitally important offices ignorant and corrupt appointees. Democracy in France has not worked well. It has not failed, perhaps, to benefit the individual so much as it has to organize the State, which lacks the power of vigorous initiative, and which is incapable of the consistent policy absolutely indispensable to prepare the nation to meet a great crisis. Surely, the destruction of more than one first-class battleship has proved with sufficient clearness the lamentable deficiency of her naval administration. The Dreyfus case proved the organization of the army to be singularly open to a type of influence which would be only too likely to be fatal in time of war. Merit, and merit alone, can be in the long run the proper test in all military and administrative appointments. It is in the selection of officials that democracy has everywhere most conspicuously failed. It could have scarcely failed in anything more vital to the protection of the State.

France, too, is no longer united. The people are courageous, unquestionably loyal, filled with ambition, but they have been growing apart as steadily as the Germans have been growing together. The German believes the forces hostile to the Republic were never stronger than at the present moment. The administration has recently succeeded in alienating the Royalists, the Church, and the Socialists; and their strength makes all three dangerous. Especially is this true in the difficulties raised by the quarrel with the Pope. The French have always been peculiarly devoted Catholics, and have more than once followed their Church rather than the State. The growth of Socialist, Syndicalist, and Anarchistic notions certainly augurs ill for the solidarity of the coming generation, or its loyalty to the Republic. A violent intestinal quarrel in France would certainly rob her of most of her offensive power, if not of her defensive strength. The Germans believe that the Republic has alienated large classes of the community, whose support will be far less warm in moments of danger than it would have been ten years ago.

France is growing physically weaker each decade. The birth rate has long been declining, and of late the number of births has shown not alone a proportional but an actual decrease. Emigration does not account for this decrease in the total population, which becomes steadily more serious each year. The most alarming aspect of the situation lies, however, in the very rapid increase of illegitimacy and juvenile crime. The Apaches of Paris were never so bold as now, and they and the juvenile criminals frankly declare their preference for a life of crime with a frequency and abandon truly astonishing. It seems, therefore, as if the newer generation which is growing up in France is hardly likely to furnish strong, steady, capable men to take the place of the generations who are passing.

Her colonial power, like England's, hangs by a thread. She has, indeed, but one valuable colony, northern Africa, where the Germans believe the natives to be so clearly dissatisfied with her rule as to render its continuance highly problematical; her commercial monopoly in her colonies is purely political; and if freedom of trade were permitted, Germany could undersell her in her own field without the slightest difficulty. Her political control, therefore, being unstable, her commercial monopoly depending upon it, the Germans do not consider it a matter of insuperable difficulty to filch from her the really valuable privilege of holding Morocco at all. The excellence of Colonel Mangin's troops and his own skill and bravery the Germans do not underestimate, but they count upon the blunderers in Paris to upset all his dispositions.

The extent of Russia's possessions, her enormous population, her astonishing growth in the last two centuries, the Germans fully appreciate. They well know that her population was twelve millions in 1700 and was one hundred and fifty millions in 1900; that her revenue of five million dollars in 1700 had become one billion dollars by 1900; that whereas she controlled in 1700 an area not much larger than Germany herself, she now controls one seventh of the land surface of the globe. Men and money she has lavishly spent in the ruthless pursuit of those same ambitions which she has to-day. To secure the Baltic cost Russia seven hundred thousand lives. Her territory on the Black Sea cost the same. In the eighteenth century she sent five million men into the field, and a similar number into the wars of the nineteenth century, and did this with a population only a fraction of that she can now command. There is small chance that she will not exert the same proportional amount of effort in the coming century in the same ruthless pursuit of the same aims. Above all, the Germans know that nothing stands between them and these multitudes of men but their own army.

They know at the same time that a nation's strength is not what she possesses, but what she can effectively use, and German diplomats are still of Bismarck's opinion that Russia's international value depends upon "a single pair of eyes," in other words, upon the Tsar himself. Russia, they claim, is too autocratic to be dangerous in proportion to her strength; the Tsar can make the alliance and with equal rapidity and ease be persuaded to break it; Russia's actions depend too entirely upon the personal opinion of her rulers and too commonly lack support in the opinion of the nation to make her a very valuable ally or a very dangerous enemy. The administration is overladen with red tape, nor can the confusion and inefficiency be lessened while her rulers insist upon directing from St. Petersburg the details of administration in so enormous an empire. Russia, in other words, is so large that centralized government is inefficient. The hierarchy in St. Petersburg cannot, in the very nature of things, possess enough knowledge about the different localities they govern to direct their subordinates successfully; they are necessarily thrown upon the mercy of the subordinates themselves, from whom they must, perforce, derive the great bulk of their information about conditions in the district, and the conduct of affairs. Such a government is necessarily blind, slow, cumbrous, hesitating, incapable of acting promptly, or of executing ably the details of a complex scheme of offense.

The Russian people are, in the opinion of Germans, too numerous, too widely separated, to have a truly national consciousness obtained by common experience in thought and action, even were they all of the same race, and even if they were all enthusiastically in favor of the Government. The educated class in Russia is capable but small, and its numbers and character have both been vitally influenced by the policy of the Tsars in restricting education to non-political subjects. In order to limit the forces against them, in order to limit the possible leaders of the subject nations, and the possible leaders of the Russian people in the war upon the dynasty, they have systematically opposed the extension of education and training, and have thus conserved the dynasty at the price of a very real loss to the nation in vital strength. Underneath the nobles are the educated and the administrators, and underneath the somewhat larger merchant class is the great bulk of the people, of whom those who are not too miserable, ignorant, and down-trodden to have thoughts beyond existence itself, are mostly irreconcilables who hate the government with an energy almost beyond conception. Their numbers are considerable and include such vitally important districts as Finland and Poland, where Germany might easily receive important assistance by instigating a popular revolt. Indeed, Russia's power can never be more than potential until she has pacified and consolidated her own people.

Financially, Russia is bankrupt, think the Germans, despite her enormous resources, for the revenues which succeed in reaching St. Petersburg (certainly a fraction only of the taxes collected from the people) are for the most part pledged to the payment of the interest and capital of the Japanese War loans. Certainly, it is widely believed that the money for another great

war could not be raised in Russia and would not
be supplied by foreign capitalists without more
securities than Russia has left to pledge. Where
so enormous a proportion of the population still
exists upon an essentially primitive type of agriculture, where manufactures are as yet in their
infancy, where the vast mineral resources are still
largely undeveloped, the available resources
within Russia herself for the prosecution of the
war are really inconsiderable compared to her
ostensible strength.

The army the Germans do not consider dangerous. The Japanese showed clearly how easily
the Russian generals could be outmanœuvred, and
how incapable the Russians were of holding even
strong positions against a determined assault
directed by real tacticians. The greatest difficulties which the Russian generals had to meet arose
from the quality of the human material with
which they had to deal. The men, and even the
non-commissioned officers, only too often lacked
sufficient intelligence to execute any movement
requiring something more than obedience to the
letter of the orders issued them. Blind courage,
the capacity to suffer hunger and cold which
would have caused the German army to mutiny,
the dull qualities of the brute, these the Russian
troops possessed; intelligence, discretion, capabil-

ity, and initiative, all these, and more, vital to so complex an organization as the modern army, the rank and file did not possess at all. An army, insist the Germans, is not a machine composed of a certain number of parts, but an organization of men which must be intelligent to be effective. It is in the army, especially, that the inefficiency of Russian administration and the lack of intelligence in the rank and file of the Russian people produce the most striking results for evil.

Russia's real destiny, the Germans believe, is in Asia, not in Europe. Her people are more closely allied to the Asiatic than to the European; her methods in government are those of the East, not of the West; her religion is Oriental, not Occidental. She is placed so as to command ready entrance into the very heart of China and India, where native administrations less efficient than hers rule a people still more ignorant. Sooner or later, Russia, think the Germans, will realize this and renounce her foolish ambitions in Europe. Needless to add, the Russians have not the slightest intention of doing anything of the kind.

The existence of France and Russia, dangerous as it is to Germany, is not without its compensations, for their positions bind to her firmly her allies, Austria and Italy, without whose help the great scheme of Pan-Germanism would be impossible of execution. To be sure, if France and Russia did not exist, the great scheme might not be necessary, but it is certainly fortunate that their existence makes simple the securing of aid. Austria, as well as Germany, lies in the path of Russian progress, not so much because of her territory in Austria proper as because of her own determination to expand into Poland and to reach the sea through the Adriatic and the Ægean. Austria, therefore, depends for the realization of her dynastic aims upon obtaining possession of the Balkans. If she should do so, the Russian plans for obtaining control of the Black Sea and for securing an exit into the Mediterranean through the Bosphorus and the Dardanelles would become impossible of execution, for even if Austria permitted Russia to obtain Constantinople and the Straits, her own possession of Macedonia and the great port of Saloniki would effectively prevent Russia from controlling the Ægean. Austria, therefore, whose assistance Germany vitally needs in the North, equally needs the help of Germany to prevent Russia from taking possession of the Balkans and thus ending for once and all her own hopes of expansion. The ambition of Russia makes Germany and Austria permanent allies.

Italy, without fears of absorption by Russia and without vital fear of invasion from France, nevertheless finds the assistance of Germany imperative for the realization of her own plans of expansion in the Mediterranean. It is obvious that to obtain colonies in Africa she must either take them with the consent of England and France, or fight the latter for them, a proceeding hardly possible in view of the preponderance of the English and French fleets in the Mediterranean. Germany and Austria, therefore, can alone enable her to obtain a position in the Mediterranean in the face of the opposition of France and England; Germany by her threats of attack upon the English fleet, Austria by actual assistance in the Mediterranean itself. In addition, Italy is well situated to assist Germany in her struggle against France by an attack upon the French rear through the passes of the Alps. She would also be in admirable position to fight Russia in the Balkans, should the latter succeed in penetrating so far, while her navy would be of the utmost importance in the Mediterranean. Indeed, the position of Sicily, the great ports at Naples and Messina, would be of paramount importance in depriving Malta, the key of the English defense, of much of its strength; and from Genoa, the Austrian and Italian fleets might together easily contest with the French at Toulon the possession of the western Mediterranean, and the Italian fleet alone, mobilized at Genoa, might prevent the coöperation of the French and English fleets by forcing the French to remain behind to protect their naval base. Should they sail, the Italian fleet could menace the rear, or might actually destroy Marseilles, if not Toulon. In short, if the Triple Alliance should ever propose to contest the supremacy of the Mediterranean with England and France, the coöperation of Italy would be indispensable. Austria and Italy could in all probability be depended upon to keep Russia and France occupied while Germany dealt with England.

CHAPTER V

WHILE well aware of the fact that the central position is, from a military point of view, one of weakness for a power compelled to defend herself, or not prepared to take the offensive, Germany is equally aware of the undeniable fact that the central position, for a power which proposes to take the aggressive, possesses enormous advantages. She can attack either France or Russia with equal ease; her army is equally ready to defend her against both at the same time, thus affording her the maximum opportunity for utilizing her men to advantage. In addition, she holds the great strategic points of northern Europe, — Alsace-Lorraine, the door to France; the Kiel Canal, giving her access to the Baltic without exposing herself to the necessity of utilizing the Sund; her allies hold the Swiss passes and the vital points affording passage into Russia and the Balkans. Everything vital to her, indeed, everything she owns, forms a compact territorial unit which can be defended by the minimum force with the maximum ease. She has no long chain of forts or

islands to guard, no great stretches of land in
Africa or Asia to protect, no subject races to
pacify like the Hindus or Moroccans. She considers, therefore, that her strategic position, far
from possessing the weakness which her enemies
believe it has, is one of such strength that it affords
her advantages which might almost be called
conclusive in the sort of a struggle in which she
proposes to engage. She is not vulnerable to attack
from a fleet; England's greatest offensive weapon
is useless against her; for, while the English fleet
could stop the passage of German commerce
through the English Channel, it is powerless to
undertake any offensive movements which could
endanger her existence. Nor could it stop her
trade overland, a trade already great in volume,
steadily expanding, and which would, with the outbreak of war and the consequent exclusion from
Europe of English manufactured goods, attain
unsuspected dimensions. Indeed, the outbreak
of war might conceivably permit German merchants to take from the English their whole market on the Continent by the very simple fact that
war would certainly close the harbors, while German goods could still cross the frontiers by rail.
Such an eventuality the Germans consider something more than a possibility.

Germany, however, looks with greatest pride

at her economic strength. She feels that she occupies in the economic world a truly extraordinary position, as one of the few nations who are still literally self-sufficing, who can even feed and clothe themselves. When she compares her population with that of England and France, she derives solid satisfaction from the knowledge that, in an area equal in size to France, she has nearly fifty per cent more people, and in an area more than one third larger than England's, she has a population one fourth larger. The number of men on whom she can call for active service in time of war will be naturally to that extent greater than those at her rivals' disposal. She is, therefore, not surprised to find that her standing army, ready to go to the front at a moment's notice, is twice as large as the English army on paper and almost four times as large as the French. When she adds her reserve army, nearly equal in size and efficiency to her standing army, she wonders how England and France can seriously consider opposing her wishes, and looks upon the outcome of any possible conflict with supremest confidence. The density of her population is 301 units as against England's 367, and France's 190; her revenue *per capita* is $10, while England's is $15, and France's is $20, proving the ease with which her people have borne and are bearing the cost of a military and naval expansion unparalleled thus far in German history. It is, however, when she looks at her public debt and compares its size with that of her rivals, that she feels most confident of the outcome of war. Her public debt *per capita* is something over $15, while England owes $80 per individual, and France carries the enormous burden of $150 per person. Germany, therefore, not only has more people and more acres, but has been able to accomplish vastly more with the imposition of much smaller burdens upon her population. Agriculture has reached a state of high perfection in Germany; manufactures have undoubtedly made great progress. Indeed, her great economic efficiency is clear from her success in competition with other nations in every field of industry; she has even beaten them in their own markets. The proof of the degree of her prosperity and the extent to which she is self-sufficing the Germans see in the fact that, while her exports *per capita* are $24, her imports are about $30, whereas England exports $40 *per capita* and imports $65.[1] Germany, therefore, is, like England, a creditor nation, and is clearly producing far in excess of the ability of her people

[1] These figures are only approximate; no really accurate figures are possible because no definitive figure can be given for the population except in a census year. That figure, too, is always inaccurate by the time it has been compiled.

to consume. This economic efficiency rests upon the solid basis of the possession within her own borders of a fairly adequate supply of most raw materials required to keep her factories at work, and, what is perhaps more essential, of all those materials peculiarly necessary for the maintenance of an army and a fleet, not excepting the most essential of all, food and iron. Nor is she at the mercy of England, as most other nations are, from the lack of a merchant marine of her own to distribute her products to the rest of the world. While her merchant fleet is new and does not upon paper compare favorably, either in number of ships or in registered tonnage, with the English merchant marine, at the same time no one doubts that in actual efficiency it can seriously be compared with England's.

Her vast resources Germany is prepared to utilize to the full. Her government is admittedly one of the most efficient in the world. Her capable bureaucracy, her local government conducted purely on scientific and business principles, her centralized imperial administration, provide her with the most advantageous methods of accomplishing the greatest results without wasting a man or a mark. The motto of German government has invariably been efficiency, the securing of the greatest results with the least expenditure of energy. To be sure, this has involved an amount of interference with individual rights and privileges which has in some cases almost amounted to the ordering of the individual's life by the government, and which has been sneeringly called, by other nations, paternalism, less, as most Germans think, because other nations dislike the results than because they despair of obtaining them. The average German is supremely satisfied with his government, and is above all pleased with the results. He feels that only jealousy can cause others to criticize.

The advantages of centralized government he feels to be great in times of peace, merely from the point of view of obtaining the most favorable results in internal administration. But the real benefits of centralized administration will be most apparent in time of war. Indeed, without such a centralized administration, the execution of any such gigantic scheme as Pan-Germanism, extending necessarily over a long series of years and requiring continuity of policy and careful preparations for eventualities known of necessity only to a few, would be utterly impossible. In England and in France, power is distributed in too many hands to make continuity of policy and vigor of administration really possible; in Russia, the country itself is too large to be directed efficiently by a single head; in Germany, the happy mean is found. The certainty, therefore, of the complete utilization of every ounce of the national strength in the struggle approaching, with nations whose governments are not able to utilize the whole of their strength, makes the Germans supremely confident of success. They are certain that they are stronger than England under any circumstances; they are sure that their resources are considerable enough to cope with France and Russia combined; and they believe that they are stronger than all three nations in the amount of force which they are capable of actually exerting.

The efficiency of administration, the possibility and necessity of continuity of policy, is most apparent in the rapidity with which the Germans have developed their army and navy to the present point of high efficiency and size. They realize, certainly to a degree no other nation does, the extent of the preparation necessary for participation in modern warfare, and the number of years of preparation indispensable to success. War, indeed, is too terrible to be invoked without the certainty of success, especially by a nation strategically situated, as Germany is, between two enemies thirsting for her destruction. The Germans realize that a successful war must be prosecuted by a highly organized machine, equipped with exceedingly expensive apparatus, officered by men whose training must necessarily consume years, during which they and the troops they are instructing must be supported by the State and allowed to devote their whole time to learning the game of war. The Germans learned long ago that a citizen army drawn from farms and counting-houses at the outbreak of war cannot be expected to understand manœuvring. It is a difficult thing for a hundred men to do something together; it is a much more difficult thing for a hundred thousand men to manœuvre without getting in each other's way; but when a million men are to be transported to a certain spot, equipped, officered, fed, and expected to execute a complicated attack with efficiency and dispatch, nothing short of a most complicated organization can even put such an army into a field, and nothing short of years of practice can possibly make it efficient.

On the other hand, the Germans realize that a weapon of this sort is not to be successfully resisted by anything less highly trained. To-day an army to repel an invader can no longer be garnered from the countryside as the invader advances, armed with weapons taken from the wall of each man's house, officered by the nobility and gentry, and by them hastily organized into companies. The same elaborate preparations which were essential to its undertaking will be required to meet invasion. War is also expensive, not alone because of the length of time the men must be in training, but because the apparatus which they must learn to use is expensive to create and expensive to practice with. A gun crew, that is to be called upon in time of danger to hit a moving mark at the distance of several miles, a mark invariably out of sight, must have had considerable practice in time of peace to be able to hit anything in the excitement of battle. The expense of firing a twelve-inch rifle is in the neighborhood of a thousand dollars, and gun crews usually are instructed to see how many times they can fire the gun in so many minutes. Preparedness for war at this rate means that the nation must pay for it gradually, which means in turn that the money must be spent over a long series of years. The Germans are certain that no other nation in Europe has spent the same amount of money or exercised the same amount of forethought or possessed the same degree of belief in the necessity for preparation that they have. Why, then, doubt of success? In fact, the preparedness for war bears to-day so inevitable and obvious a relation to the result of the combat that actual fighting is likely to occur only between forces that are apparently equal in size and efficiency. The Germans hope to make their army so large and so competent that it can decide contests without appearing in the field.

Germany's greatest strength, however, lies, as her rulers think, in the hearty coöperation of the German people in the great scheme. They seem all to be willing to sacrifice and suffer whatever may be necessary for the realization of the great vision which has already enthused the nation for so many years. The government will be able to count on the active, willing coöperation of the whole people in the prosecution of any plans which may be deemed necessary for the preparation or the execution of this project. The Socialists, despite their hostile theories and speeches, have pledged themselves to play their part like men when "the day" dawns. Indeed, the very things which make expansion necessary for Germany's future are those things which will be her greatest assets in promoting the war and the most certain gauges of her success. Her rapidly growing population, her busy factories, the swelling volume of product, these are the very tools with which Pan-Germanism is to be built. They are the pledges fortune has given Germany of its realization; their existence furnishes Germans with all necessary proof of the expediency and morality of the course they have adopted.

CHAPTER VI

ENGLAND AND FRANCE AS THEY SEE THEMSELVES

WHILE it is hardly expedient to interrupt the exposition of Pan-Germanism in order to interject a complete consideration of the factors upon which England and France are depending for their own salvation, it is indispensable to make clear at this point some facts of their national development which give them confidence, and, above all, to describe in detail their economic position, for it is upon what they consider to be the elements of its greatest strength that Germany is counting to compass their downfall. In their own eyes, England and France have had a truly glorious past. They have been for at least three centuries the leading nations of Europe, France being the model during the seventeenth and eighteenth centuries for language, literature, fashions, to say nothing of administration; England becoming in the nineteenth century the model upon which the rest of the world diligently strove to form itself. The Napoleonic Administration and the Napoleonic Code have had an

extensive influence, say the French, in the formation of modern Germany; the English point out
that the centralized government of which Germans are so proud is, after all, nothing but an
adaptation of the English parliamentary system.
France feels that but for her support the Catholic
Church would hardly be what it is in Europe
to-day; the English are more than positive that
their support alone kept Protestantism alive.
In science and literature they consider themselves
not less preëminent. Surely, say the English, the
doctrine of evolution is the most significant element in modern thought and the most purely English; truly, say the French, Voltaire, Rousseau,
and the Encyclopædists directed the thought of
the world into new channels which it has not yet
found inadequate. The industrial revolution, the
new agriculture, the factory system, trade-union-
ism were all begun in England. If Germany is
great, her greatness rests upon foundations laid by
England and France. They ask the Germans to
point out one conspicuous achievement in which
they have not at least shared. Nor do they fail
to derive comfort and satisfaction from the contemplation of the extension of their policy in the
modern world. England controls one fifth of the
total land area of the globe, one fifth of its total
population; half of North America, a quarter of

Asia, and nearly half of Africa are under her flag; while France may point with pride at the possession of a dominion in Africa, vast in extent and rich in resources. Certainly, there are no two nations in the world which control so large a share of its surface, its population, or its resources. Compared to what they hold, the Steppes of Russia and the vast frozen dominion of Siberia are valueless. In addition, the whole world governs itself on the English model; the whole world wears French clothes; the only two languages which have any claims to universal use, since Latin ceased to be the language of the learned, are French and English. Even if they should grant the truth of every statement made in pursuance of German greed as to their strength and position, these great cardinal facts must make it evident, they feel, that the German argument possesses some flaw which will not be less fatal because it is not obvious.

England and France feel, however, that, even if they were politically and strategically as weak as Germany believes them to be, they have still a tower of strength in their economic supremacy, based upon natural advantages whose potency cannot be denied. The conspicuous features of recent economic growth have been the interdependence of nations, the extension of the credit system, of international trade, and the rise of such huge aggregates of capital as the Rothschild fortune. The growth of the nineteenth century has made commercial development depend on the production of something which others need, which one nation makes better than others or produces more easily, and which that nation can exchange for those products naturally and easily produced by others. The old ideal of a people entirely self-sufficing has disappeared, not because it was bad in its effects upon the people, but simply because it has become clear that no single people can profitably devote their time to producing everything they need. The economic interdependence of the world has progressed with such rapid strides because it has proved more profitable to all nations than the earlier system. The truly progressive nation to-day will, therefore, not expect to be self-sufficing, and will abandon the industries in which it is not specially fitted to surpass by natural conditions or by its skill.

The credit system of international exchange, by which vast transactions are accomplished without the passing from hand to hand of even tokens of value, has entirely altered the methods of transacting the world's business and has increased the extent and profitableness of this interdependence. Moreover, out of the factory system and modern industry have grown huge aggregations of capital, available for immediate use and controlled by comparatively few men. There are individuals in the world to-day who themselves control revenues greater than those of many nations, whose incomes annually at their disposal are as large as most of the fortunes of antiquity. They thus may wield stupendous power in the development of nations. Indeed, modern business depends upon the possibility of utilizing such enormous aggregations of capital for the promotion of single enterprises. The English and the French make no idle boast when they claim that the modern economic structure, national as well as international, has been largely their creation and is now largely in their hands. Of certain staple materials, like wool, fur, fish, they practically possess a monopoly; in London and Paris are the centres of the world's exchange and credit system; to London and Paris bankers accrue the profits of handling the world's business.

Nothing short of a financial panic of the first magnitude, accompanied perhaps by the dislocation of all business traditions, can fail to result, they think, from the disarranging of these dispositions. The English yearly produce an enormous bulk of manufactured goods which has steadily increased in volume at the rate of from ten to

twenty per cent each decade. England is steadily growing richer and not poorer, as the Germans
insinuate. The French monopoly on such luxuries as jewelry, dress goods, and most articles of
personal apparel is as complete to-day as it ever
was. The world's carrying trade is practically in
English hands and its profits are no small share
of the English national wealth. Any one who
supposes that the English merchant marine could
be annihilated without dislocating the commerce
of the world is either exceedingly misinformed or
intentionally blind. London and Paris are, furthermore, the distributing centre for Eastern and
African goods, for which the demand was never
greater than it is at present. How is it possible,
say the English and the French, for the world to
get along without us? Is it in any degree cred-
ible that Germany can take our place, can rearrange the whole financial and commercial structure of the world, without causing an amount of
suffering to herself which would more than coun-
terbalance any possible benefits she might receive?
Indeed, the English and the French are not altogether unreasonable in supposing themselves at
present indispensable to the economic welfare of
the world.

The interdependence of the world, moreover,
which is so profitable to every one concerned, is

absolutely contingent upon the continuance of peace. Every one will be injured by the inability to exchange what they produce for what they need. Anything like a general war will necessarily entail financial loss, and not improbably personal suffering, upon the individuals of practically every community in the world. It is, therefore, the peace advocates strenuously insist, to practically every one's economic advantage to maintain peace. The number of individuals, to say nothing of nations, who would be likely to gain by the outbreak of war are too few to be regarded, and consist, they claim, chiefly of those who make the materials or the weapons needed by armies and navies. These facts, indeed, are sufficiently apparent to furnish a solid basis for great organized movements in favor of international arbitration or conciliation, whose propaganda is so active, and whose logic and statistics are so unassailable, as to have convinced the great majority of every-day people in all nations of the inexpediency of war. Unquestionably, such movements and arguments, tending to the maintneance of a *status quo*, are greatly to the advantage of England and France, in whose hands lies the present control of the financial world.

The greatest economic strength of England and France comes from their possession of the greatest individual aggregations of capital in the world. The vast Rothschild fortune, known in Europe as *The Fortune*, is one twentieth of the total wealth of the French nation, and is not, like so many American fortunes, the estimated value on the stock market of certain securities which, in case of a financial panic, might almost lose all value, but consists of houses, land, railways, solid tangible assets which could be destroyed only by the destruction of France. In London, there is a group of individuals who between them control nearly as considerable and almost as solid fortunes. There are no doubt in Germany and Austria wealthy men. There are no such fortunes as these. In fact, the London and Paris bankers can almost control the available resources of the world at any one moment, and can therefore practically permit or prevent the undertaking of any enterprise requiring the use of more than a hundred million dollars actual value. Many schemes nominally more considerable than this have been floated independently, but the actual value of the assets behind the scheme was a mere tithe of their value on paper.

Modern warfare means that the degree of preparation essential to success is impossible without the use of immense resources, and that the nation can safely invest enough money in

armies and navies to make them effective only
when it boasts vast reserves of capital. The English and French consider it almost impossible for
any nation to invest such a sum in war without
straining its resources far beyond the danger
point, or without somehow borrowing it from
them, and they will certainly not loan it to their
enemies. Therefore, they conclude, if Germany is
thus investing her surplus, the time will come
when her armies will cost her more than they are
worth, — indeed, more than the utmost success in
war could ever enable her to repay. Actually to
mobilize a modern army requires vast sums in
ready money, and the English and French do not
believe any nation can go to war without procur-
ing the ready money from them. The conclusive
proof of this supposition they found in the event
following the appearance of the German warship
Panther at Agadir. It seems that the Emperor
would have been willing at any rate to mobilize
the German army and sought the German bankers with a request for a loan to the Government.
The bankers informed him that they had no
money with which to meet their own pressing
obligations and that the nation as a matter of
fact stood on the verge of bankruptcy. Not only
could it not go to war, it was doubtful even
whether it could continue to do business for an-

other week. No one seems to have realized in Germany the sum total of the private loans made in London and Paris. When war seemed probable, a concerted movement by the London and Paris bankers for the recalling of all loans practically stripped Germany of ready money, and the sale of securities on the Berlin Bourse to meet these demands almost precipitated a panic of the utmost seriousness. It transpired that Germany was conducting nearly ninety per cent of current business upon borrowed money subject to recall at a moment's notice. By the use of their economic weapons, England and France rendered Germany helpless and made war impossible. It is clear that in the present era there are weapons stronger than armies.

Not only does the credit system of the world centre in London and Paris, but the world's supply of the only tangible basis for international exchange is also in their hands. From South Africa comes a large share of the world's gold; in the London and Paris banks are probably the world's greatest accumulations of coin and bullion, while probably there are in France greater sums of cash in the hands of the nation itself than in any other country in the world. When the close of the Franco-Prussian War imposed upon France a war indemnity so heavy that the Prussians exulted openly upon their success in crippling France for a generation, the French nation produced the entire sum from its savings, and paid the indemnity with a rapidity which astounded the world. The French are undoubtedly more capable of repeating such a feat to-day than they were in 1870. Such financial strength rightly inspires the French and English with confidence in their ultimate ability to cope with Germany.

It is an astounding fact, of whose truth the average man is gradually becoming conscious, that England and France own probably the major part of the bonded indebtedness of the world. Russia, Turkey, Egypt, India, China, Japan, and South America are probably owned, so far as any nation can be owned, in London or Paris. Payment of interest on these vast sums is secured by the pledging of the public revenues of these countries, and, in the case of the weaker nations, by the actual delivery of the perception into the hands of the agents of the English and French bankers. In addition, a very large share, if not the major part, of the stocks and industrial securities of the world are owned by those two nations and the policies of many of the world's enterprises dictated by their financial heads. The world itself, in fact, pays them tribute; it actually rises in the morning to earn its living by utilizing their capital, and occupies its days in making the money to pay them interest which is to make them still wealthier. Such facts as these are of transcendent importance in evaluating the conditions in the world which make war possible or impossible. In the estimation of the statesmen in London and Paris, Germany is not economically strong enough to utilize what she thinks is politically and strategically an advantageous position without involving an injury to herself which might ultimately destroy her prosperity.

In fact, they find it difficult to believe that Germany possesses any economic strength. The factors which the Germans consider favorable to them, the English and French consider their greatest weakness. Germany's imports somewhat exceed her exports and create the impression to the superficial observer, say English and French experts, that she is a creditor country like England, receiving more than she gives, and therefore undoubtedly solvent. In this case the statistics are misleading. Germany's imports are not really the insignia of wealth at all, but are the proof of national poverty. The balance in international trade, as every economist knows, is paid in goods and not in money. The English imports are vastly in excess of exports, because England is really a

creditor country and is thus receiving the interest
owed her upon her investments. But Germany's
surplus of imports is not interest payments upon
her own investments, but payments to her of the
capital of her own enormous loans. She receives
the sum in goods, because only in kind can great
exchanges of value between nations take place;
she pays the interest with her exports. Germany
is in truth economically weak, and in order to
finance so many public and private enterprises,
as she has in the last thirty years, has been compelled to borrow heavily. In fact, in an economic
sense Germany does not own her own business.
The capital which created it, the ready money
which keeps it alive, are both borrowed and are
not yet paid for. Instead of devoting a part of
the proceeds of the use of this capital to the dis-
charge of a part of her capital indebtedness, she
has reinvested all of it, has therefore expanded
her transactions at a rate all out of proportion to
the amount of business she was really doing, and
has therefore exposed herself to the peril of being
called upon suddenly to pay her debts and of
being forced into national bankruptcy because of
her inability so to do. Such financiering is simply
folly, to the thinking of England and France.

The small national debt of Germany, too, cannot fairly be compared with the large national

debts of England and France as a sign of the comparative strength of the three nations. She owes her debt mostly to them. They owe their debts to their own citizens. A nation's position in the international scale is not affected at all by the existence of public indebtedness which is owed to its own citizens, because the total national assets are comprised of the public funds plus the actual assets of all individuals, including all the debts owed either the nation or its citizens by other nations or their citizens. The public debts of England and France are for the most part national assets, while Germany's is almost entirely a national liability. If the English and French should pay their debt, they would pay it to themselves. In other words, they would merely alter the form of recording the national wealth on the national books. When Germany pays her national debt, she will have to part with actual value which will accrue to other nations. Nor do the Germans seem to realize that, from the point of view of international finance, the national debt is not the money which the nation has borrowed in its own name, but the total amount of indebtedness which the nation itself and all its citizens combined owe in any way to all other nations and their private citizens combined. The public indebtedness plus the private indebtedness is the true indication of the money which the nation may be called upon to pay. England and France, publicly or privately, owe very little money outside their own borders. Germany owes money in every quarter of the globe on the transactions of her citizens. For these reasons, other nations find it hard to believe that Germany possesses any economic strength at all, and therefore find it difficult to understand why she promotes such vast schemes of aggression. They can be prosecuted only upon borrowed capital and must inevitably increase her inherent weakness. Certainly, should she lose, she can hardly recover from the catastrophe for a century; and they cannot see how she can possibly win.

CHAPTER VII

THE GERMAN VIEW OF THE ECONOMIC SITUATION

GERMANY freely admits the great economic strength of England and France, *so long as peace prevails*. Once war breaks out, their economic strength will become weakness and the position, which they depend upon to secure for them control of the world, will in very fact bankrupt them. Indeed, the weapons, in what the Germans are fond of calling " The next war," will not be confined to armies and navies, nor do the Germans consider that the state of war will be confined to actual hostilities. To their thinking, the war is already in progress and is being fought and will continue to be fought, with those weapons, infinitely more deadly than cannon and small arms, economic crises. They propose to destroy England and France, not in the field, but in the counting house and in the factory, annihilating the basis upon which in the long run armies must depend for maintenance.

The interdependence of the world is economically profitable to England and France, so long as the existence of peace gives full scope to the play of economic forces which produces that steady and uninterrupted interchange of goods upon which they rely for their very existence. The extent of modern economic development, the amount of produce they depend upon receiving from abroad, the amount of manufactured goods that they depend upon exporting yearly, is the measure of their economic weakness at that moment when a state of war makes the transportation by sea of their necessities dangerous. In particular, England must be fed from oversea, and must bring from a distance all the raw materials which she needs to keep her factories in constant operation, and which she must have to keep her great population steadily employed and able to support itself. This dependence upon others is not strength, but weakness of the most vital description, for it makes England's prosperity contingent upon the continuance of certain conditions which the Germans are by no means willing to agree are normal or natural. They deny strenuously that peace differs from war in anything except degree. There is a large school of thinkers in Germany who insist that all living is war, and that upon the continuance of this battle the healthy life of the community absolutely depends, in support of which assertion they cite the doctrine of evolution in its varied forms and phases. If this be true, a nation which expects to survive in this normal struggle for existence must not depend upon fighting its battles with other nations under what are really technical limitations. By depending upon the absence of anything like physical force in the struggle for existence, England is building her house upon the sands.

Take, too, the vast capital of whose existence England and France are so proud and upon whose operations they depend for the perpetuation of their predominance. The fact that they have invested it in every quarter of the globe, intending, thereby, to protect themselves from too considerable loss in case war should break out or countries become bankrupt, has actually forced them to part with the reality of their wealth and to substitute for it unreality. They have placed the tangible results of their investment the width of the globe distant from their shores, and therefore from their armies, and they have taken in exchange a promise to pay, which they do not possess the force to exact, and whose whole value depends upon the willingness of the debtors to consider it binding and to liquidate the debt of their own free will when it becomes due. They have invested their money everywhere except at home, and have therefore exposed themselves to its loss, because their ownership of these debts and investments depends on the continuance of the present notions of commercial morality. This is not investment. This is speculation. The reality, — the railways, factories, mines, — which represents the capital they have invested, belongs literally to the borrower. He has the only tangible thing in existence in the world, the only thing which possibly can exist in the world, as the equivalent of that value. Whatever is written on paper is paper, and is not to be made into factories or railways or tangible assets of any kind by any process of jugglery such as the mediæval bishop performed when he baptized the roast and called it carp. Things *are*, and writing on paper does not change the thing or its position. The real wealth of England, the surplus of which she is so proud, comes not from her soil nor from her own factories, — in other words, from those things which no one can take away from her except by force of arms and which she necessarily protects as long as she continues her national existence, — but from her income from the accumulations of the past with whose actuality she has parted, and from which she has received for decades the payments represented by the excess of her imports over her exports. The world has paid her tribute, but the world need continue to pay that tribute only so long as it wishes. The moment the borrowers refuse longer to recognize the validity of her claims upon their revenues and incomes, and begin to realize that they hold, with a clutch which she cannot loosen, the actual substance of wealth, then they will begin to see that her wealth is not real, but depends purely upon their willingness to continue to pay her revenue, which they may stop paying her at any moment without suffering any consequences. To be sure, such notions as these presume the violation of every notion of commercial morality and expediency at present existing in the world, but, as the Germans say, *if they were violated,* what could England and France possibly do to avert destruction. It is true, they admit, that such a wholesale repudiation of debts would undoubtedly make it difficult for nations to borrow from each other for some time to come, but, they retort, if such a repudiation took place, the debtor nations would not need to borrow money for generations to come.[1]

[1] The author is anxious to state explicitly that these paragraphs are not to be understood to imply a reflection upon German national or individual morality, and he hopes that, in his desire to put this hypothetical case forcibly, he has not given it an immediate application, which, if believed, might be construed as a serious prediction of a nature which no historian has a right to make. The point upon which the Germans insist is, what would happen to England under such circumstances, a statement which by no means argues their intention to attempt the repudiation of their debts to-morrow or at any other time. They do claim that it is a fundamental point in their favor.

THE ECONOMIC SITUATION

Now if we suppose that the German fleet should secure control of the sea, either by defeating the English or by securing predominance in number, it might promptly cut England's communications with the rest of the world and effectively bankrupt her by stopping the remittances of goods, in which alone the debts owed her by other countries can be paid. Germany, to be sure, would not get the property England owns elsewhere; she might not be able to secure the repudiation of English debts by England's debtors; but she could quite as effectively compel England to lose the only tangible evidence of ownership and forego the payment of the incomes of thousands of her private citizens who would infallibly be ruined. In this connection, the Germans eagerly claim that, if a nation's debts consist of the national indebtedness plus the private indebtedness, it is not less true that the nation's resources are the national revenues plus private incomes. If the latter should suffer severely, those upon whom the Government chiefly depends for the payment of taxes would be unable to respond and the nation, as well as its citizens, would be bankrupt. To secure so stupendous a result as this is well worth the expenditure of money for building a fleet. That money so far as the German nation is concerned is merely in-

vested in an enterprise from which they confidently expect returns perhaps one hundred fold.

As was said at the beginning of this account of
Pan-Germanism, the Germans are acutely conscious that their position in the world depends
less upon the actual force they are prepared to
exert and the actual wealth within their own
borders than upon their ability to exert more than
their rivals can. The existence throughout the
world of a state of war they believe would effectively bankrupt England and France. Each nation which owed the latter money would be unable to remit the usual sums, because they would
be forced to spend the money, and more likely
the goods already in existence, upon preparation
for war. This would effectively rob England and
France of their incomes, of the only tangible evidence they receive of their vast nominal wealth.
Failing to receive the usual remittance either in
money or in goods, they might themselves be
unable, simply from the lack of materials, to
prosecute the war with the vigor and dispatch
they intended. Of course, should England retain
control of the sea, she would be able even in time
of war to protect the remittances to her; but the
Germans depend upon their fleet to interfere, at
least with the regularity of remittances to England, and depend upon their allies and upon the

necessities of various nations elsewhere to stop the remittances at their source. They thus hope to cripple England and France temporarily by the mere force of economic factors which could be put into operation by simply beginning a war.

The Germans claim that those financial factors, which seem to be weaknesses in time of peace, would be in case of war a tower of strength. Germany is almost, if not quite, self-supporting, and, with the trade between herself and other European nations overland in time of war, she could become entirely self-sufficing. Nor is she dependent upon her imports for the raw materials to keep her factories busy or to maintain her army and navy. Whatever the balance may be upon the books of the world, she is actually rich, actually richer than England or France. So long as her army is unbeaten, no one can take away from her her factories, mines, and fields. Whoever may own them on paper, she owns them in reality and will continue to own them so long as she is strong enough to keep them. Supposing now that she should repudiate the whole debt which she owes other nations, should seize the capital out of which her economic development was created, what then? Would she not actually possess her economic development for nothing? Could she ever be compelled to pay for it by anything short of actual conquest, and is there in the world any nation strong enough to subdue her upon her own soil? Would not such an economic blow destroy her enemies with greater certainty than any conquest by sea or land? Indeed, has she not everything to gain from war and nothing to lose? So long as peace prevails and she continues to recognize the validity of present notions of commercial morality, she must continue to pay huge sums, must continue yearly to part with actual wealth in goods until the debt is paid. The moment war breaks out, she need pay nothing. If she is defeated, she will merely be compelled to pay what she was already obligated to pay. If victorious, she need never pay interest or principal. Would that not be a stake many times worth playing for, compared to a war indemnity of any size whatever, and, when such a manœuvre might also not improbably compass the control of the world's commerce, what German would doubt that the chances of war are better than those of peace? Suppose, too, that the rest of the countries who owe money to England and France should adopt Germany's tactics and seize the occasion of the war as a signal for the repudiation of what they owed, and should therefore take possession of their own industries; would not England and France be literally destroyed, reduced to the acres within their own boundaries and to those few industries which they could prosecute without coöperation from other nations?

The securing of ready money with which to begin this war the Germans do not consider a vital difficulty despite the fact that it must be in some way secured from their enemies.[1] Nor do they consider it a vital difficulty that they can in all probability procure only from the same source the sums of money necessary for the completion of the preparations for war. So long as the trusting citizens of England and France are willing to lend their private fortunes on no better security than the promise to pay interest and capital at some future day, there is every reason why she should continue to borrow every cent they are willing to lend, for by that measure will she increase the extent of the ruin which may in time overtake those nations, and by that extent will she increase the amount of wealth which she may get for nothing. She has, of course, continued to reinvest in her businesses the whole profits which she has derived from her skillful management, and she has not made as yet extensive prepara-

---

[1] There is a war reserve in gold in the Fortress of Spandau which the Government acknowledges contains 140 millions of marks. It is more than probable that this is to be kept as a last resort in case defeat should make the defense of Germany itself necessary.

tions for sinking funds to pay the principal of her debts, because she may not need to pay that principal. Every debt makes her stronger, every loan makes her enemies weaker. She is well aware that many of her private citizens have invested money in other countries, that she, too, is entangled in the network of international investments, but she knows that the profits will still be enormous, even if her citizens lose every penny they have invested outside her borders. She will get the cash with which to begin the war by borrowing from her enemies, and she will this time either commandeer the money in the banks before war is declared, or she will make war too quickly to permit any repetition of the manœuvre executed by the London and Paris bankers in the summer of 1911. She cares very little who claims title to that money, so long as she has it, so long as they can take it from her only by force. She is conscious that German securities will everywhere fall in the foreign stock exchanges when war actually begins; she also knows that English and French stocks will tumble likewise, and, she believes that when the reaction of economic forces is complete, the destruction of values in England and France will be too great to make the loss of value in her own securities of any significance. Besides, who own her securities? Who, therefore, will bear the fall in value? Her securities are only paper. The factories and fields they actually represent are not changed in value by operations on the stock market. The foreign investor will lose money and will bear the only ostensible losses and will thus be dealt an additional blow. Germany, in other words, can fight her enemies with their own money, and may obtain not only her industries for nothing, but her army and navy and the whole cost of the war as well. The foreigner may even provide her with the money necessary to begin the war.

Once more the Germans hear around them outcries against the morality of this procedure. Once again the Germans insist that morals and ethics have nothing to do with this particular issue. The moral code of the financial world, like the moral code of the political world, is based upon the notions of England and France, upon ideas obviously themselves the result of a peculiar situation, on whose continuance the welfare of England and France depends. Their moral code is based on their ownership of the world and their desire to continue it in perpetuity, and their moral code, therefore, condemns Germany to insignificance. The Germans refuse to recognize as moral anything which jeopardizes their national existence. They claim the right to protect themselves by any weapons which will secure the desired result, and they have no intention of foregoing the use of these terrible economic weapons, simply from a supine acceptance of so-called ethical notions, whose very presumptions militate against them. The international economic situation chances to press less heavily upon Germany than upon other states, and thus affords her a significant natural advantage over other states which it would be suicidal to forego. If worst comes to worst and all else fails, she can resort to weapons so powerful as to destroy her adversaries.

CHAPTER VIII

PREREQUISITES OF SUCCESS

BEFORE so vast a scheme as Pan-Germanism can be actually put into operation many prerequisites will be necessary to insure its ultimate success, for Pan-Germanism aims at obtaining for Germany and her allies control of the world and at insuring their retention of that control for at least a generation. The absolute prerequisite is necessarily the creation of a great fleet, large enough to insure freedom of passage of German commerce through the English Channel under any and all circumstances. The fleet must be large enough to make dubious the outcome of a battle with the English fleet, in order to prevent England from risking battle. Germany, in sooth, does not intend to use her fleet for war. It is a purely defensive weapon, intended to insure the continuance of the position she now holds and of that freedom of passage through the Channel, which is the prerequisite of all expansion. Until that is assured the possession of colonies, the entrance to markets, the ability to manufacture, are all worthless. She must not permit herself to remain in a position where the outlet for her commerce depends upon England's good will. She intends to create so large a fleet that it will command, as a matter of right, what Germany desires. Furthermore, unless her fleet is large she will not be able at the same time to intimidate England in the Channel and Russia in the Baltic. Unless she can maintain her control on the southern shore of the Baltic, all of the normal outlets for the commerce of North Germany might be closed by Russia, and it is almost as essential to insure their freedom from Russian interference as it is to make sure the English will not close the Channel. Germany wishes nothing which she must hold on sufferance. Again, if the Germans do not succeed in building their fleet fast enough actually to endanger England's predominance in the Channel, they may still compel her to concentrate her fleet in the North Sea, and leave necessarily exposed to the attacks of Germany's allies the long chain of forts and strategic places upon which England depends for the protection of her water routes to Asia and Africa.

No less necessary than a great navy is a great army, large enough and efficient enough to prevent Russia and France by reason of its existence from thinking of war. The army is, as the Germans claim, primarily defensive. It is the only

102

barrier between Germany and her enemies. It takes the place of the English Channel, of the Alps, of the Pyrenees. The army, too, must be large enough to enable Germany, in case of war, to invade England without so much exposing herself to France and Russia as to invite assault from either or both. Indeed, it is highly essential that the army should be so efficient that there could be no doubt of its repelling a combined attack from both should they take the offensive. But sufficient strength to discourage them from fighting is even more desirable from the German point of view, for the Germans do not wish to fight. They wish to secure the results of war without the concomitant disadvantages, and they consider as the only probable offensive use of the army the necessary invasion of England. Again, an army large enough to make possible such movements would also be large enough to put into operation the economic factors, which Germany expects will prove so advantageous to her and so fatal to England and France. Hence, every step in the development of such an army is a step toward the achievement of Germany's purposes by that type of offensive weapon euphemistically known as peace.

The seizure of Belgium and Holland will very likely be the first German movement when the actual accomplishment of Pan-Germanism seems fairly assured. The position of these two countries, their wealth, and the traditions of European policy have gained them so much prominence and have caused all nations to attach so much importance to them, that Germany will certainly not take possession of them until the last moment. Indeed, it has been so long held that an attack upon the autonomy of Belgium or Holland would be the equivalent of a declaration of war upon Europe that Germany will certainly avoid any such outspoken manifestation of her intentions. Notwithstanding, their position is an absolute prerequisite of the ultimate success of Pan-Germanism, and the railway lines for landing troops in the proper places are already built and the canals for supplying those troops with food are already being dug. When the German Emperor recently visited Belgium a remark was made by a certain dignitary that Belgium was prepared, to which he is reported to have replied, that they were wise to prepare.

But Germany needs the strategic points which those two countries control. The Netherlands alone can furnish her a suitable naval base on the Channel from which to contest its possession with the English or from which to intimidate the English fleet into permitting German ships complete

Conceivably there might thus be created a nexus between the two nations which might permanently bring about some relationship freeing them both from the spectre of war. The annexation of the Scandinavian countries would also put into Germany's hands beyond a peradventure the great supplies of iron, coal, and wood which the outbreak of war would make far more valuable than their intrinsic worth in time of peace. Nor does she forget that Denmark still owns a valuable colony or so in the West Indies, which would be worth her while. Some arrangement with Switzerland would also be necessary, although its exact nature could only be indicated by the exigencies of the moment. Napoleon's phrase that Switzerland was the key to Europe the Germans constantly bear in mind. Through Switzerland an attack could easily be delivered upon the German rear by France in case of war. Germany or Italy might profitably utilize it themselves for an attack upon the French rear, while the Austrians have not forgotten that a military road to Vienna runs through Switzerland. However, Germany's arrangements with Switzerland will probably be made rather to prevent the utilization of the Swiss passes by others than from an expectation of utilizing them herself.

A most essential part of the structure of Pan-

Germanism is a confederation of states in the Balkans either outwardly independent and secretly controlled by Germany or Austria or dependent in some way upon Austria or Italy. The great stretch of mountain, tableland, and valley, extending from the heights of the Tyrolese and Transylvanian Alps to the Ægean and the Mediterranean, has long been loosely designated, from political rather than geographical reasons, the Balkans. It boasts no real geographical unity and has been divided for political reasons into so many different entities at so many different times that it is in reality from every point of view nothing but a geographical expression. At the moment of the conception of Pan-Germanism, the states of this region were partly autonomous, partly in the hands of Austria, and partly controlled by Turkey. The creation out of them in some way or other of some kind of an entity or entities, which the Triple Alliance could keep under its control, is absolutely essential to the success of the most striking part of Pan-Germanism. For in those defiles and valleys are the keys to Europe. Down along the coast of the Black Sea runs the great road from Russia to Constantinople and the East; down the Danube valley, across the river at Belgrade, through the Balkans by way of Sophia and Adrianople, runs the great continental highway, trodden for a thousand years by Roman, Barbarian, Crusader, Infidel, leading from the Rhine and Danube valleys to Constantinople and the East. Round through Macedonia and Albania runs the perfectly practical road, used long ago by the Visigoths, leading from Constantinople to Trieste, Venice, and the valley of the Po. At Saloniki is a great port from which a fleet might control the Ægean. The western side of the Balkans is the eastern shore of the Adriatic, and its possession would insure to the Triple Alliance complete control of that important sea. Could they secure, therefore, by controlling the Balkans, possession of the great roads between Europe and Asia and of the strategic positions necessary for controlling the Ægean and the Adriatic, the English position in the Mediterranean might be made untenable. At any rate, the English so-called Protectorate over Turkey and Greece would be at once terminated, and the possession by Italy and Austria of naval bases in the Adriatic and the Ægean would practically render useless all the English dispositions based upon Malta as a centre. Thus the Triple Alliance would secure a foothold and probable control of the eastern Mediterranean, and would throw back upon their base in the western Mediterranean the English and French fleets, and might be enabled without practical interference

to take possession of Egypt and "Suez." Even if
so much were not accomplished, the trade route
overland through Constantinople into the neutral
territory of Turkey, and so by way of the Baghdad
Railway to the Persian Gulf and India, would
be a reality, and it would be unassailable by the
English fleet, nor would it ever be exposed to those
dangers which so constantly threaten the English
Empire with dissolution.

Chiefest of all, however, the existence of the
Balkans, their geographical position, their racial
and religious character, their traditions and history, would furnish Germany with the necessary
prize to offer Austria as the price of her assistance
in the execution of Pan-Germanism. The rulers
of Austria have long seen that her expansion to
the north and east was improbable and undesirable; that her expansion to the west was permanently blocked by the Alps, and that she could
only expand to the south along the great plains of
the lower Danube and Black Sea, down through
the valleys of Servia to the Ægean, and to the
southwest to the Adriatic. Like all other nations,
she sees the permanent assurances of her continued national existence only in the possession of an
outlet to the sea, and a possible share in the commerce with the less developed parts of the world,
from which her rivals are so rapidly obtaining

wealth and position. She early found in the Balkans no less powerful a rival than Russia, one as determined as she to secure similar opportunity for expansion, and one to whom that opportunity is not less essential than it is to her. Between the two no compromise is possible. Austria may keep Russia out of the Balkans, but in the face of Russian opposition she cannot unaided take possession. The necessary assistance, Germany and Italy proposed to afford her through the execution of the great schemes for the aggrandizement of all three.

With the Balkans in their hands, the reorganization of Turkey would be the next essential step. Its undeniable importance is the result of the very factors which have kept the Turk so long in possession. In the past, Europe considered its many strategic points too valuable to be owned by any nation not so inefficient and weak as to render their use improbable. The incurable malady of the Sick Man alone caused the doctors to allow him to live. First of all, Turkey holds the bridge between Europe and Asia, for whose possession throughout the centuries Roman and Barbarian, Christian and Infidel, had so vigorously fought. The Turk also holds Asia Minor, from whose rich fields Rome had drawn a vast revenue, whose roads lead into the great vales of the Tigris and Euphrates, where in antiquity stood the greatest of the old empires. In Asia Minor, too, are marts of trade from which Phœnician and Greek cities almost without number had grown rich and powerful and cultured. The whole North African littoral owes allegiance to the Sultan; Tripoli was still nominally administered by him, and would furnish to the Turk's master a strategic point of the first consequence, flanking Egypt on the one hand and Tunis on the other, furnished with harbors whence a fleet might assail with confident expectation of success the English lines of communication with Suez. Above all, the Sultan is head of the Mohammedan religion, ruling still over the countless hordes of Moslems in the English and French possessions in Africa and Asia, to whom they owe implicit obedience and for whose safety they have often evinced the utmost concern. Indeed, around him is already centering the great movement known as Pan-Islam, which contemplates nothing less than the expulsion of the unbeliever from the lands of the Prophet's followers by a great Jehad of unheard-of dimensions. Might not the Sultan, properly "inspired" in some way, be induced to instigate or proclaim such a war at a time when English and French authority in Africa and Asia might for all practical purposes be extinguished by it? An outbreak as general and as powerful might conceivably compel them to send reinforcements from Europe to such an extent as to weaken them at home and permit Germany to begin the final stages of the war with every prospect of complete success. Naturally, Germany does not expect to receive everything and give nothing. She has undertaken the reorganization of Turkey, the building of an army and a navy adequate for the prosecution of such enterprises, and she has, as a matter of course, provided the necessary financial backing to relieve the Turk of pressure from his old supporters, England and France, and from all future fears as to deficits.

From the Turk could be secured the railway concession of vital commercial importance which should join Constantinople with the Persian Gulf, and whose existence would alone repay Germany and her allies for all their expenditures and risks. It would, of course, be adequately protected by the new Turkish army and fleet. To insure its safety from an attack by Russia, Persia would be reorganized as an independent nation under the German ægis. Thus also would be secured the coast road along the Persian Gulf to India which Alexander had followed, thus also would be insured to Germany the control of navigation in the Gulf itself. Both would put into her hands invaluable points. She would be led by the coast road into the valley of the Indus behind the great defenses at Quetta; in the rear, therefore, of the British position. A fleet emerging from the Gulf would enter the Indian Ocean behind the English naval defenses, and see all India lying before her, undefended.

The Germans do not fail to appreciate that, although they are the originators of Pan-Germanism and may perhaps not unreasonably expect to be the chief gainers by it, they cannot hope finally to achieve success without the hearty coöperation of Austria, of Italy, of Turkey, of Persia, and, above all, of the Balkans. They realize that these states will by no means enter a conflict of this magnitude out of love for Germany; that they are not likely to be held to any agreements that they may make by a moral sense of obligation, which the Germans themselves frankly deny is of any validity in international agreements; that, unless they are fully satisfied with their own gains, they will themselves interfere at some awkward moment and perhaps prevent the completion of the scheme at all. Therefore, the ultimate success of Pan-Germanism will depend as much upon the division of the spoils when the victory is won, as upon any single factor, and upon the acceptance beforehand of such plans for the allotment of territory as to satisfy the ambitions of the various parties without vitally offending any other equally essential party. *Divide et Impera.* In all probability, Austria is to get the Adriatic, access to the sea through the Balkans, and Egypt and Palestine; Italy will certainly expect the rest of the North African littoral, while the Balkan States, European Turkey, and Persia will insist upon a guarantee of their autonomy so far as their own local affairs are concerned. Germany, therefore, will surrender the Mediterranean to her allies in exchange for India, the rest of Africa, and the East and West India Islands. Spain might have to be paid with a slice of western Morocco. Whether or not the coalition will be strong enough to lay its hands on South America in defiance of the United States will have to be determined by the circumstances of their victory.

CHAPTER IX

FIRST STEPS

WHEN the historian leaves the consideration of schemes and plans and undertakes
even to sketch the course of events in current history, he finds himself in the peculiar position for
a historian of being overwhelmed with details of
whose meaning he is by no means certain. Indeed,
he is continually exposed to the danger of assuming that all events have some meaning and that
particular events are of necessity those truly
significant. While the archives remain closed
and the diplomatic correspondence a sealed book,
while the real answers to all those questions he
most anxiously asks are known only to a few dis-
tressingly discreet men, he can hardly do more
than indicate the main features of current politics,
which seem, after mature consideration, to have
an absolutely unavoidable connection with the
execution of this great scheme. Indeed, the historian is in that extraordinary position, true of no
other epoch in history, of knowing the plans far
more certainly than he does their execution. He
must in matter of fact be constantly prepared,

always with due caution, to interpret facts, which he frequently does not understand, by means of the schemes which he definitely knows to be in the minds of statesmen. Nor is there possible in modern history anything like a clear demonstration of the truth of any single proposition by the line and precept familiar to investigators in other fields. In the nature of things, final proof of the truth of any single assertion is impossible, and will continue to be impossible for certainly two generations and perhaps a century. The historian, therefore, is forced to do the best he can, and must be more than chary of attempting to deal with anything except the broadest outlines of the story. Exactly what relation to its broad outline any single series of events may have, is impossible to indicate with accuracy, and the reader must be aware that the historian is not attempting to give him certainties, but is forced to give him statements which would be considered, in treating any period of past history, conjectures, but which are, in current history, literally the best we have.

The authorship of the great scheme which we call Pan-Germanism is least of all a matter of certainty. There seems to be little doubt that it was the product of German thought and of German interests, but no student of current affairs can believe for a moment that important aspects of it were not the result of the views and interests of Austria and Italy. Bismarck was the first statesman to see all its possibilities, though we are as yet unable to be certain how much of what is now called Pan-Germanism he is actually responsible for. Von Bieberstein, Von Tirpitz, and above all the present Emperor, are responsible for much, and certainly deserve the credit (or discredit) of bringing the scheme to its present state of perfection. The date of its origin [1] is an even more perplexing question, and could be more definitely settled if we were sure that events of the past generation were all steps in the development or furtherance of the same scheme and not of two or three schemes, out of which the exigencies of times and occasions gradually developed the present Pan-Germanism. The historian, who wishes to be cautious, is inclined to take the latter view and to conclude that Pan-Germanism is an outgrowth of the various policies advocated by German statesmen after the formation of the present empire.

The creation of the fleet, whose existence at present is without doubt one of the definitive elements of Pan-Germanism, was probably, as the Germans claim, not as vital a part of it as we

[1] Cecil Battine, in the *Fortnightly Review,* xci, New Series, 1056, 1057, places the beginning of Pan-Germanism between 1893 and 1895. Article 4 of the Constitution of 1871 indicates that colonies were foreseen at the very beginning.

might easily suppose. As has already been said, the German looks upon the fleet as the only means of insuring to Germany the continuance of her present position, unfavorable as she considers that to be. The fleet is essential, not so much to assist her expansion as to make positive her existence. In all probability there have been three phases of German policy: the first, an attempt to secure colonies; the second, an attempt to obtain entrance into the markets of the East by the establishment of a trade route across the Balkans and Turkey, which formed by international agreement a neutral zone; and thirdly, the determinedly aggressive scheme for the actual forcible conquest of the world. Exactly when the one gave way to the other, exactly which of the many events in recent history belong to one and which to another, is difficult to indicate with anything approaching accuracy.

During the decade between 1880 and 1890, an extended effort was made to obtain in various parts of the world suitable colonies for German expansion. The land not already occupied by European nations was inconsiderable in area, unfavorably located, thinly populated, and not possessed of obvious commercial advantages; but such as was available Germany occupied, not because she deemed it adequate provision for her needs, but because, at the moment, she saw no other chances for meeting the exigencies which she knew were certain to arise within a decade. The colonies thus founded on either coast of Africa and in the South Seas speedily proved their unsuitability for colonization by white men, and the improbability of their affording before the lapse of a century anything like an adequate market for German manufactures. To be sure, these colonies were in area nearly a million square miles, but their products were not greatly in excess of five dollars value for each square mile, a sum too absurdly inconsequential to be mentioned. The population of about fourteen millions was too undeveloped and too sparse to make the creation of a state possible. All the desirable land for colonies, as a matter of fact, was already in the hands of other nations, and the Germans realized with bitterness that they had been able to secure what they held, simply because other nations had not considered it of value. It was clear that the execution of any schemes for German expansion would involve interference with other nations.

The next attempt, probably only one of several, seems to have been a variation of the well-known European method of taking possession of other people's property, called peaceful penetration.

The nation, proposing to absorb a district and make a colony out of it, loans money to the ruler and to as many of his subjects as possible; obtains as security for the money advanced, if it can, a part of the public revenue; builds railways in exchange for large grants of land, and, in general, "develops" the country. Then, when the available resources have been pretty completely hypothecated, the nation claims that its interests in the territory are so considerable that it must be conceded a share in the direction of administration and policy, in order to insure the safety of its investment. A little study of the situation soon convinced the Germans that the French influence in Morocco, the English influence in Egypt, the English and Russian influence in Persia, and the influence of the United States in Central America were due precisely to these methods, and the Germans saw no reason why they should not "peaceably" penetrate some one of the South American nations, by pleading the same highly moral purpose of developing the country for the use and behoof of its inhabitants, who were, of course, to be assumed incapable of developing it themselves. After some hesitation, they seemed to have pitched upon Venezuela as the most favorable scene of operations. They succeeded in placing some large loans, in buying some mines, and in initiating a number of business enterprises, and, then, in most approved fashion, descended upon the Republic, anchored a warship in its harbor, and made the stereotyped demand for some share in the control of its administration. Of course, the rest of the world promptly saw the trend of German policy, and, with equal promptitude, realized its objective; the United States, as the nearest country, invoked against Germany a new variety of the Monroe Doctrine, and informed the disgusted Germans that they would not be permitted to interfere in the government of Venezuela. They certainly could not afford peaceably to penetrate countries unless they were to be allowed to enjoy the profits of the enterprise. Besides, they became aware, with rather painful force, of the fact, which they had no doubt always known, that they could obtain access to such a colony in the Gulf of Mexico, while England and the United States controlled the Atlantic Ocean, only by the permission of those two nations, both of whom indicated with considerable firmness their distinct dislike of Germany's proposed action.

The Germans turned their eyes, therefore, to Africa, and in particular toward the great temperate district of South Africa as a zone becomingly fitted by nature for the use and behoof of the white race. The temperate climate, the presence of the great diamond mines, of deposits of gold in all probability huge in size, the certainty of the profitableness of agriculture and cattle-raising, offered enticing prospects for the successful development there of a great colony, which would provide a considerable market for German goods and would raise products of its own with which to pay for them. German Southwest Africa would afford a basis from which to act in case they should ever desire to take the offensive, but the existence of the Boer Republic made it probable that it would not be necessary for Germany herself to take the field; she could much more easily and profitably act through the hands of the Boers. The strained relations between the latter and the English simplified the problem of producing a *casus belli* for a war which might easily result in robbing England of a most valuable colony, which Germany might succeed in annexing. In addition, the project boasted the double advantage of testing the strength of the British Empire, its defensive ability, the loyalty of its subjects, and, whatever the result might be, the information, which the war would certainly afford Germany, would be well worth the money and arms she would have to furnish the Boers to get them to begin it. Supposing that the war should succeed, should reveal, as the Germans believed it would, the disloyalty of the English colonists in South Africa, should make clear to all Europe the weakness of Imperial England, the moral results would be without question stupendous. Its success, even if it should result in creating a Boer state too strong for Germany to interfere with, would cut the communications between the Cape Colony and the vast estate of Rhodesia, which lay adjacent to German East Africa, as well as to German West Africa, and which could then easily be annexed without danger and without cost. To be sure, it would be necessary to train the Boers in modern warfare and to equip them and furnish them with funds, and there was always the danger that England would discover the fact prematurely and take action before the Boers or Germany herself should be ready. However, some risks were inevitable.

The Boers took kindly to the idea. The immigration of Englishmen into their territory, the rapid expansion of the English colonies to the north and south of them, had shown them clearly that their own expansion was problematical, because the Uitlanders were multiplying by immigration at a rate vastly in excess of the natural increase of the Boers and at a rate which made it a certainty that many years would not elapse before the Boers would be outnumbered to so great an extent that their real power would disappear. From their point of view, the preservation of their autonomy depended upon action before a further increase of strength to the Uitlanders should make action impossible. Every year's delay only reduced their chances of victory. Moreover, they were promised bountiful assistance and all the supplies they should need. There is little doubt they fully intended in case of victory to defy Germany as well as England, and, if possible, cheat her of all the advantages she had hoped for. Conscious of the issue, England exerted herself to the utmost and inflicted upon the Boers in the end a crushing defeat. Not so much the wealth of her South African domain excited her as the determination to make manifest to Germany and the world the strength of her imperial bond. Her prestige she realized must be maintained at any cost, not only because of the conclusions which her subject peoples in India and Egypt would draw from a defeat, but because of the conclusions which European nations would draw. She simply could not afford to be defeated; the loss of the war might precipitate a general alliance of all Europe against her. To the amazement of the Germans, England was able to finance the war without too much effort, maintain an army in the field whose efficiency, even under new and adverse conditions, was astonishing, and which was supplied, equipped, and reinforced from England despite the distance between Southampton and Cape Town. Every nation in Europe knew that England had performed a feat which it could not perform, and had demonstrated a degree of executive and military efficiency for which no one had given her credit. The still more crushing defeat of Germany and her schemes for weakening the British Empire was accomplished by the formation of the South African Union, in whose federal bond are comprised all the varied peoples of South Africa, and in which the Boers have taken their place with singular success. So far as can be seen by foreign observers, so far as can be told from the statements of the inhabitants, the tact of the English administrators has pretty completely settled the grievances of the various elements of the European population, and has gone a long way toward solving the perplexing race issue, caused by the presence of so large a number of the natives.

German statesmen, thus thwarted, gave up, so far as can be learned, for good and all their designs upon South Africa, and turned their attention to the much more feasible scheme of constructing an overland route to the Persian

Gulf. Germany and Austria very well knew that
they did not own the territory stretching from
their own borders to the Persian Gulf, and that
they could not hope to take possession of it in the
face of the international determination to preserve its neutrality. They counted upon this very
neutrality as the basis for their scheme of building
a railway from Constantinople to Baghdad. To
relieve the fears of England and Russia, they did
not propose to locate its terminus actually upon
the Persian Gulf. After some difficulty and nego-
tiation, the concession was secured from Turkey
and the acquiescence of the international concert
was obtained. It is not certain, but it is highly
probable, that at this time the real purpose of the
railway was not suspected in London or in St.
Petersburg. However that may be, the loan for
its construction was underwritten in Berlin and
the building of the railway was begun in sections.
The details of construction are hardly of consequence here, and it suffices to say that the last section of the road is just about to be begun. After
work was well under way, England and Russia
realized its purport and began to consider operations in Persia which should effectively prevent
the railway from doing anything more than develop Asia Minor.

Thwarted thus at every turn, German statesmen found themselves fairly driven to adopt the comprehensive aggressive scheme which we now call Pan-Germanism. They began its execution at the point of least resistance and by methods so far as possible of a neutral nature. The fleet was already under construction; the railway was rapidly being built; the obvious step to take was the peaceful penetration of Turkey as the necessary preliminary for assuring Germany the continuance of the concession. Turkey, as every one knew, was weak, disorganized in every way, and nothing could be more natural than an attempt by the Sultan himself at the proper administration of his own country and the adoption of financial measures which would insure the payment of his debts and his household revenue. The Sultan eagerly accepted the secret tender of German assistance in the accomplishment of such extremely desirable ends, and began, apparently upon his own initiative but really under German direction, the reorganization of the army and navy, the reorganization of the finances of his empire, gradually introducing German officers into the important positions in the state. Men were appointed governors of provinces to introduce local reforms calculated to diminish the amount of racial warfare, the friction between the soldiery and the populace, and to minimize

the difficulties arising from the old struggle between the Latin and Greek Churches. Gradually,
Germany insinuated herself into the confidence
of the Young Turk party, already long in existence, and whose main aim was to cast off the
foreign rule which had so long pressed hardly
upon the Turk and had drained his country of
its resources for the satisfaction of foreign debts
for whose making the Turk himself was not responsible. Eventually, by means of the agitation
undertaken by the Young Turks, organized by
the Committee of Union and Progress at Saloniki,
a revolution was accomplished (probably with
the connivance of the Sultan), a constitution was
adopted, a new Sultan took office, responsible
government began, and Turkey was thus freed
from the treaty obligations made by the older
régime, which had given every nation except Germany some obvious interest to defend and therefore some obvious right to interfere. If Germany
was to base her scheme of Pan-Germanism upon
the control of Turkey, she must certainly control
it by means of a government owing its very existence to her. The price of the support of the Turks
was to be the autonomy of Turkey in local government, and protection from the interference of her
old "friends."

Meanwhile, the Germans diligently investi-

gated the condition of affairs in the Balkans, in
Morocco, Persia, Egypt, and India. They found
in all a native party of some considerable strength
and vigor, which had already had continuous existence for a decade or more, and whose main
object was the obtaining of autonomy and the
exclusion of the foreigner. Those parties had been
nourished upon the democratic literature of the
Occidental nations, had been fired with enthusiasm for self-government by the spectacle of parliamentary and republican government in Europe
and in the United States, and, in fact, had assumed that no small share of the prosperity of the
Western nations and the greater part of their
strength were due to their form of government.
The natives saw that it would be profitable and
pleasurable for them to govern themselves, or,
as a cynic would be more inclined to put it, for
them to govern their less progressive countrymen.
In these subject countries of Europe, Asia, and
Africa, the power so long in control had been
alien in race and religion, had long systematically sacrificed the interests of the people to the
assumed exigencies of international politics, and
had placed upon the country heavy financial
burdens for the production of a revenue which
the people themselves were not allowed to spend,
and for which few natives considered that the

people even received an equivalent. In Africa,
Asia Minor, and Egypt the majority of the people
were Mohammedans, who had long chafed under
the control of the Infidel, and who were only too
ready to enlist in a movement for a change of
government, which would possess the sanction
of a religious crusade. The ground, therefore,
was ready for the Germans, and the tools to till
it were at hand.

In the Balkans, a peculiar admixture of races
and religions had produced a singularly complex
situation, in which the various forces reacted
upon each other with continually surprising results. At the same time, so far as the people themselves were concerned, the two great issues were
religious, — the survival of the crusade of the
Christian against the Turk, and, on the other
hand, of the still older quarrel between the Latin
and Greek Churches. From both of these counts,
as well as on many national and racial issues, dis-
content was rife, and could in all probability be
turned to political advantage by Germany and
her ally, Austria. Above all was this probable
because the most evident enemy, the oldest and
the worst hated enemy of all the Balkan peoples,
was the Turk, whose rule over them had long
furnished them with practically the only sentiment they had in common, a vigorous hatred of

the Infidel. Now, when Germany should have reorganized Turkey and have gotten the Sultan, and the administration, to say nothing of the army and navy, well into her hands, what would be simpler than for her to permit the Balkan nations to begin this war under her direction, and thus secure their gratitude by the realization of the ideals cherished for so many centuries? Would it not also be easy to satisfy in the most thoroughgoing manner their oft-repeated demands for the freedom from oppression of their co-religionists in Macedonia and Albania? It seemed highly probable to the Balkan nations that they could not fail to be gainers by an alliance of this sort, and, while they hesitated, like the man in the fable, to admit the camel to their tent, they fully realized that the German offers did not present them the alternative of rejection. Should they not see fit amicably to come to an agreement with Austria and Germany, they would not unlikely run the risk of absorption by force at some future time, when they would certainly not receive such favors as the terms suggested. Like the Trojans, they feared the Greeks even when they came bearing gifts; but, if it was dangerous to accept the presents, it was more dangerous to decline them. Under any circumstances, they did not see that money, munitions of war, military instruction by German and Austrian officers, assistance in the fortification of their own country could be so very undesirable, and it was as clear to them as it was to their new friends that such weapons would be susceptible of more than one use. Indeed, the weapons and instruction were of themselves a guarantee of their new allies' good faith.

In Morocco, the Germans found an even more favorable scene of operations. They learned that the Sultan had governed regularly by forming alliances with part of the tribesmen against the rest. By clever diplomacy and the occasional use of money, he had managed to keep them jealous of one another and prevented their uniting against him. His main dependence, nevertheless, was the existence of an army of mercenaries whose size was distinctly limited by his own poverty. The French had come to his rescue and had provided him with a highly trained force of really remarkable soldiers, sufficiently numerous to keep him in the ascendency. The tribesmen looked upon the presence of the French, therefore, with anything but favor, for they saw that the latter were rapidly making it possible for the Sultan to defy the tribesmen even if united, an eventuality which certainly meant the coming of an era vastly different from the age of license and rapine to which they had so long been accustomed. On general grounds, therefore, they welcomed the advances of the Germans, scenting probably presents of money or arms, and suspecting that the latter might aid them to restore the conditions to what they had been before the French interfered. The rapacity of the Sultan, his anxiety to collect the uttermost farthing due him, the imposition of new taxes from time to time, and, above all, the actual exercise of force for securing obedience gave the tribes only too ample evidence of the excellent basis for their fears. The new French native regiments, moreover, conducted themselves with a license unbecoming soldiers and aroused against themselves the hatred of the people. So considerable was the number of such cases that they formed one of the chief excuses for German interference. Nor did the Germans forget that an army as large and as extraordinary in quality as the French force in Morocco might become a distinct factor in a European war. They would therefore be making no mistake in providing this army with too much work in Morocco to permit its departure.

In Persia also the Germans made good headway. The opposition on national grounds to the encroachments of England and Russia was considerable, but lacked a definite aim and capable organization, and the revolutionary party lacked the necessary money to finance a revolt. The money, the Germans were more than willing to provide in exchange for a reasonable prospect of success. The English and Russians speedily perceived the trend of the German plans, and, as the Baghdad Railway added mile after mile in the mountains of the Caucasus and the sentiment in favor of Persian independence grew more and more outspoken, they realized the necessity of some action. They therefore sent a commission to study the situation, who reported, with grave irony, that the Persians were incapable of self-government, and suggested that England and Russia should interfere to prevent the longer continuance of the existing state of anarchy. In 1907, England and Russia acted in accordance with the commission's recommendations, and two zones of influence were demarcated, one in the north in which Russia should predominate, and the second in the south along the Gulf where England was to be supreme, and a neutral zone between them whose affairs the Persians were to be allowed to direct with such interference as England and Russia combined might see fit to interpose.

The Powers could certainly have taken no step which would have done more to strengthen the German plans. The evident insult to the capacity of the Persians resulted in a national movement of the capable men in the country, who executed promptly, with German assistance, a *coup d'état* in 1909, by which Persia was entirely reorganized, a constitution adopted, a new Shah chosen, and the administration and finances of the country put into the hands of foreigners, whose experience in government and in business was expected to teach the Persians how to conduct their own affairs, and, what was equally important, to put the new government on its feet financially. The most important of these officials was the Treasurer, an American named Shuster, whose energy, ability, and firm belief in the expediency and desirability of Persian independence, accomplished wonders. To be sure, Germany had not quite looked for the establishment of a firm, well-organized, and really independent national state in Persia; there can be little doubt that she had expected to supplant England and Russia in Persia by means of an ostensible revolution; still, the creation of a Persian government, really strong enough to exclude Russia and England, would be almost as advantageous to her as the exercise of control herself.

Progress in sowing the wind in Egypt and India

was also considerable. In both, to be sure, she found a native movement among the Mohammedans favoring Pan-Islam and the exclusion of foreigners, and which was therefore anxious to put an end to English influence and administration. It seems to be exceedingly doubtful whether Germany ever contemplated anything more in Egypt and India than the creation of trouble for England. Certainly, any promises of actual assistance to the malcontents could hardly have carried weight. The knowledge, which she certainly did impart to the leaders, that forces were at work in Europe tending to undermine the English position, that there were European states who believed England weak and who sympathized with the peoples she ruled, that before a not too distant day England might be racked by the torment of a great war in Europe, all seemed to the Hindus too good to be true. It certainly meant that England would be unable to devote all her attention to suppressing revolts in India, and that it behooved them to prepare themselves for the dawning of the day, when they might practically obtain their independence for the asking. This news put vitality into the movement of Pan-Islam. It is not beyond the bounds of probability that German money was an important factor in this vitality, money which she probably

137

borrowed with characteristic nonchalance in London.

By the year 1910, therefore, the work was well under way in all directions for the creation of Pan-Germanism.

CHAPTER X

THE SIGNIFICANT POSITION OF THE UNITED STATES

ONCE the magnitude of Pan-Germanism dawned on the English and French diplomats, once they became aware of the lengths to which Germany was willing to go, they realized the necessity of strengthening their position, and therefore made overtures to the United States, which resulted, probably before the summer of the year 1897, in an understanding between the three countries. There seems to be no doubt whatever that no papers of any sort were signed, and that no pledges were given which circumstances would not justify any one of the contracting parties in denying or possibly repudiating. Nevertheless, an understanding was reached that in case of a war begun by Germany or Austria for the purpose of executing Pan-Germanism, the United States would promptly declare in favor of England and France and would do her utmost to assist them. The mere fact that no open acknowledgment of this agreement was then made need not lessen its importance and significance. The alliance, for it was nothing less, was based upon infinitely firmer ground than written words and sheets of parchment, than the promises of individuals at that moment in office in any one of the three countries; it found its efficient cause as well as the efficient reason for its continuance in the situation, geographical, economic, and political, of the contracting nations which made such an agreement mutually advantageous to them all. So long as this situation remains unchanged, there is little likelihood that the agreement will be altered, and there is no possibility whatever of its entire rejection by one of the three parties, least of all by the United States.

The United States occupies a strategic position defensively strong, but offensively weak. She is beyond question invulnerable to the assaults of foreign fleets and armies. To be sure, her seacoast is vast in extent and for the most part unprotected. It has been truly pointed out that the Japanese might successfully land an army upon the Pacific Coast, or the Germans land an army in New York or Boston practically without opposition. *Sed cui bono?* The strategical and geographical conditions of the country on either coast are such that a foreign army would occupy the ground it stood on and no more. The British discovered in the Revolutionary War that the occupation of New York, Boston, and Philadelphia put them no nearer the military possession of the continent than they were before, and that marching through provinces was not subduing them. However seriously the capture of New York might cripple our commercial and railway interests, the difficulty, even at its worst, could be easily overcome by shifting the centre of business for the time being to Chicago, and the possession of New York would certainly not permit a foreign army to conquer the country, even if it were possible for any nation to maintain an army so far from its real base of supplies in Europe. The possibility of invasion is made of no consequence by the simple fact that no foreign nation possesses any inducement for attempting so eminently hazardous an enterprise. The United States possesses literally nothing which any foreign nation wants that force would be necessary to obtain, while, by making war upon the United States, she would certainly expose herself to annihilation at the hands of her enemies in Europe, who have patiently waited for decades in the hope that some one of them would commit so capital a blunder. But this very invulnerability of the United States prevents her from becoming a dominant or even an important factor in European politics. If European nations cannot menace her with armed reprisal or with wars for conquest, she is equally incapable of menacing them. The fact, which has been from her own standpoint heretofore an unmixed blessing, which has allowed her people to beat their swords into ploughshares and their spears into pruning hooks, becomes her greatest weakness, once she is filled with an ambition to play a part in the affairs of the world.

Unpalatable as the fact may be, the international situation, the close balance of power between the Triple Alliance and the Triple Entente rather than the position of the United States has made her a factor in international politics. Indeed, if we would be truly accurate, we must admit that the inter-relation of the various parts of the European situation, more even than its delicate balance, makes the United States a factor; for the complexity of the problems of no one group of states, whether in Europe, in the Middle East, or in the Far East, could possibly allow the United States to play a prominent part. In each, the natural antipathies counteract each other. Only the fact that every nation is anxious to maintain or win power or wealth in Europe and Africa and Asia makes the United States of any value to any of them. Indeed, it is only as European questions become themselves factors in the larger problems of India, Morocco, and the Mediterranean that they can concern the United States at all. As soon as European politics became world politics and Asiatic and African problems became European, the United States began to be a factor in their solution. She has, to be sure, no vital stake in any one of these fields. She cannot, even if she would, risk in war the same stake European nations do, her independence; the Atlantic on the one side, the Pacific on the other, defend her more completely than could fleets and coalitions. Nothing short of the creation of world politics by other nations could make the position of the United States of consequence at all. The most vital fact, however, about the European situation is that no nation possesses the same natural allies in all parts of the world. England and France are one in opposing the extension of German authority in Europe; but nothing short of their extreme danger in the Mediterranean at the time of the Crimean War and the perils to which they have been exposed in Europe since the Franco-Prussian War has buried the enmity resulting from deadly strife in America and, especially, in India. Russia is the firm ally of both England and France in Europe; she is their deadliest foe in the Black Sea, in Persia, India, and China; yet, to oppose Germany, we see Russia and England amicably enough uniting in the Near East. Germany must secure French and English aid to defend herself permanently against Russia on the east, but finds her natural allies against Russia her greatest competitors in trade, and the most determined opponents to her expansion on the west. Nevertheless, at the very moment that we find Germany and England ready to spring at each other's throats in Europe, we see them guarding the railway to Pekin together and acting in concert about the Chinese loans.

The variety of the interests of these nations makes it impossible for them permanently or entirely to trust or distrust each other. England, who needs Russia's aid in Europe in the Near East, cannot act too determinedly in opposition to Russian advance in Afghanistan and Manchuria. Germany, whose quarrels with Hapsburg and the Pope fill the history of the Middle Ages, must have their assistance to protect herself in Europe. In all this the United States has unquestionably no part. Not her strategic position, not her military strength, but her economic position makes her an ally particularly indispensable to England and France. Not their economic position but her desire for colonies, her ambition to play a part in the politics of the world, makes an alliance with England and France indispensable to the

United States. But she can enter world politics only with the consent of European nations.

The economic position of the United States in the modern world is commanding. Her area is so vast and its productivity so great, her natural resources so nearly unlimited and so great in variety, that scarcely a country in the world, one had almost said no continent in the world, can hope to rival her. While her population is not yet numerous enough to make her dangerous, it is none the less amply sufficient to render her in potential military strength one of the greatest of civilized countries. She possesses, in fact, precisely what England and France lack — almost inexhaustible natural resources; arable land almost without limit; food sufficient to feed all Europe; great deposits of gold, copper, iron, silver, coal; great supplies of cotton sufficient for the Lancashire cotton mills; in short, she possesses the very resources needed to make the economic position of England and France fairly impregnable. Allied with her, they could not be starved into submission nor bankrupted by the lack of materials to keep their looms running. In addition, she possesses the second greatest steel manufactory in the world, which owns the patents and secret processes upon which Bessemer steel depends, a product surpassed for war materials only by the Krupp steel. The width of the Atlantic effectively prevents any interference by European Powers with the continuance in time of war of her agricultural and industrial activities. Whatever happens in Europe, she can continue to produce the raw materials and finished products they need, and, what is more important, she will furnish them in time of war a huge market for the sale of such manufactured goods as they can continue to make.

The United States, furthermore, is the third financial power in the world. Not only is her wealth vast, not only is her surplus capital considerable, but the organization of business has, most fortunately from the point of view of international politics, concentrated the control of the available capital for investment in the hands of comparatively few men. The trusts, the banks, and the insurance companies have made available for investment huge sums, only less in size than those controlled in London and Paris. It is highly essential that Germany should not be allowed to establish relations with any such capital. It would provide her with precisely that financial backing which she needs. At all costs the United States and Germany must be kept apart. England, too, is anxious to turn this capital into her own colonies, and is willing and anxious to invest her capital in the United States, for both would gain from this mutual dependence, and each would furnish the other fields for investment on whose reliability they could both depend. The English are naturally anxious to shift their investments from Germany to some country where they will not be exposed to destruction by war or to confiscation based upon war as an excuse.

Fortunately for England and France, the United States, whose economic assistance is positively imperative for them, finds their assistance equally imperative. In the first place, the United States depends upon the English merchant marine to carry her huge volume of exports, and, should she not be able to use it, would suffer seriously, even if the inability to export continued only a few weeks. Again, a market as certain and as large as that of England and France for her raw materials and food is absolutely essential to her, and the outbreak of a war, which might close those markets to her, would precipitate unquestionably a financial crisis, whose results could not fail to equal in destructiveness the effect upon private individuals of a great war. The United States has come to realize, as have other nations, that there are many ways in which a modern country can be forced to suffer which are as deadly and, in many cases, more deadly than invasion. Furthermore, she needs a market in England and

France for her own manufactured goods, and has grown to depend upon receiving from them in return many varieties of manufactured goods. She simply cannot afford to take any chances of losing her markets in those two countries, nor has she ceased to hope for privileges of some sort in the English and French dependencies, which other nations do not have, and which, should worst come to worst, she could undoubtedly obtain from them as the price of her continued assistance. It is perhaps no exaggeration to say that the prosperity of the United States so much depends upon the preservation of her relations with England and France that in time of war only an alliance with them would save her from almost certain bankruptcy.

England and France, however, expect to retain the alliance by permitting her to fulfill her ambitions for control of the Gulf of Mexico. Ever since the days when Louisiana was first purchased, the men of the Mississippi Valley have dreamed of the extension of the sway of the United States over Central America and the Gulf. Aaron Burr's expedition aimed probably at the creation of an empire out of the Mississippi Valley and Mexico. The Mexican War was certainly fought in the expectation that valuable territory in the Gulf might be acquired into which slaves might profitably be carried. When the war failed, a filibustering expedition led by Walker, with connivance of the authorities at Washington, was intended to secure for the United States possession of one or more of the Central American countries. There was also the scheme, in whose existence the North believed previous to the war, for the conquest of the whole Gulf of Mexico and the creation there of a slaveocracy whose wealth and independence could easily be assured by the production of cotton, sugar, and tobacco. All these schemes met a determined resistance and interference from England and France which invariably proved decisive. Nor could the United States hope to take possession of lands separated from her coast by water, with which she could communicate only by sea, so long as the English fleet controlled the seas and she herself possessed no fleet at all. The Clayton-Bulwer Treaty was intended to prevent the acquisition of influence in Central America by the United States without England's consent, and mention was specifically made of a canal across the Isthmus of Panama. The interference of Germany in Venezuela, the evident fact that the concentration of the English fleet in the Channel would make it impossible to keep a sizable fleet in the Gulf of Mexico, the absolute necessity from many points of view of preventing

the acquisition by Germany of land in South or
Central America, removed the objections England and France had hitherto possessed to the
extension of the influence of the United States in
the Western hemisphere.

There was, furthermore, a likelihood that Germany would in some way attempt the annexation
of the oldest of European colonial empires, held
at this time by one of the weakest and most decadent of European states. The Spanish colonies in
the Gulf of Mexico and in the Philippine Islands
possessed not only commercial but strategic importance. The wealth of Cuba and Porto Rico
was proverbial, the products of the Philippines
considerable, and, though not altogether suitable
for colonization, they would afford Germany undeniable opportunity for expansion. Moreover,
Cuba in the hands of Germany would rob Jamaica
of all naval importance and might actually permit
Germany to overrun the whole Gulf. The Philippines as a matter of fact controlled one whole
side of the China Sea and contained valuable seaports, where a naval base could be established,
safe from assault by the Chinese or European
nations. The islands were thus ideally fitted to
become Germany's base of operations in the Far
East. To allow such places to fall into her hands
might entail consequences whose far-reaching

effect no statesman could possibly imagine. Nor
was there the slightest guarantee that by an unprovoked assault Germany would not attempt to
take possession. At the same time, the general
European situation and the position of Spain in
the Mediterranean made it impossible for England or France to undertake a war with her, without setting fire to a train of circumstances whose
eventual results might be even more fatal than
those they were attempting to prevent. The colonial aspirations of the United States, her anxiety
to share in the opening of China to European
enterprise, her traditional hope of securing control of Cuba, all pointed to her as the natural
guardian of the interests of the coalition in the
Gulf of Mexico and in the Far East. Whether or
not it is true, as some assert, — a view to which
certain events lend probability, — that the Span-
ish-American War was created in order to permit
the United States to take possession of Spain's
colonial dominion, certainly such was the result
of that war. To be sure, the relations between
Spain and the United States were already strained;
popular sentiment was aroused by the conditions
in Cuba, and, if the war was "created," it was not
a difficult task. Certainly, Germany and her allies
suspected that such was the purpose of the war,
and attempted to secure a general agreement in

Europe to interfere in Spain's favor. England, however, whether because she saw its advantage now the war was in existence, or because she had caused it to be begun, decisively vetoed the suggestion of interference, and her control of the sea made action without her coöperation impossible.

The results of the war were all that could have been hoped for. The Triple Entente saw the Gulf of Mexico fall into friendly hands and the establishment in the Far East of a friendly power in the strategic point of greatest consequence. From Germany's point of view, the results of the alliance between England, France, and the United States were exceedingly discouraging, and the aftermath of the war proved even more decisive than the war itself. The United States promptly undertook the peaceful penetration of Mexico and Central America. Large loans were made to the governments and secured by a lien on the revenues; American capital rushed thither, and the number of enterprises financed or owned by Americans increased so rapidly that at the present day the United States, or its citizens, owns practically everything of importance in the Gulf, and is waiting only for a favorable opportunity to foreclose its mortgages. The possibility of German interference has been reduced to nothing. The United States also proceeded, not improbably by agreement, to create a fleet large enough to maintain control of the Gulf of Mexico and, what was of more consequence, to maintain control of the Atlantic highway between Europe and America in case of European war. The English had come to realize the improbability that enough of their fleet could be spared to patrol the seas in the event of an attack upon their forces in the Channel or in the Mediterranean. Above all, the United States undertook to create in the Philippines a naval base of sufficient size and importance to permit the maintenance there of a fleet large enough to be a factor in the Pacific. England and France obviously could not spare enough ships to maintain a fleet in the Far East; Japan would not tolerate the presence of a Russian fleet in those waters; the United States was the only member of the coalition who could, consistent with her own safety or that of other nations, undertake the creation and maintenance of such a fleet in the Far East. She became, in fact, the offensive arm of the coalition in the Pacific, and promptly strengthened her position by annexing the islands between her shores and Asia available for settlement or coaling-stations. She must not only prepare the way for the further extension of the coalition's power in the Far East, but she must prevent the acquisition by Germany of colonies, whose location or development would interfere with the control of Eastern commerce by herself and her allies.

One more thing the United States undertook, which England and France had hitherto denied her permission to do, the digging of the Panama Canal. The canal would furnish the United States with a new waterway to the East, shorter than the route she had hitherto been forced to employ *via* Suez, and with a route which would literally put New York in actual number of miles nearer China, Australia, and New Zealand than was London. Thus to admit the United States to the trade of the Far East by a waterway exclusively in its control, England had not hitherto considered expedient. The creation of Pan-Germanism, the fear of an attack on the English route through the Mediterranean and the Suez Canal, the possibility of the closing of that route temporarily or permanently by some naval disaster, reconciled England to the creation of the Panama Canal, because she saw in that waterway a new military road which she could use to her own possessions in the Far East, and which the Atlantic Ocean would effectually keep out of the hands of Germany. To be sure, it would not be as short a road to India as that through the Mediterranean and Suez; but so far as Australia and New Zealand were concerned it

154

would not be longer; and all such objections inevitably were reduced to insignificance by its incomparable safety, so long as the English fleet could hold the seas at all. So long as the United States and England combined could maintain control of the Gulf of Mexico and of the islands in the Pacific, so long would this waterway be absolutely safe. If, then, Germany should succeed in executing the whole of her stupendous plan, England and her allies might still be able by means of the Panama Canal to contest with her the possession of the trade of the East. Especially would this be true if the United States should be able to maintain herself in the Philippines. Nor have the English lost sight of the incomparable importance of the Philippines for keeping Germany out of the Celebes. If Germany should move upon Holland, the coalition expects to take possession of the Celebes without further ceremony, and will then hold a position controlling the trade routes leading from India to China and Japan and to Europe in general, which would be as nearly impregnable as anything of the kind ever yet known in the world. The issues, therefore, with which the United States is actively concerned are vast; the importance of her adhesion to the side of England and France cannot be overestimated, and her possible part in the movements of the next two decades is certainly one which ought to satisfy the most ambitious. She holds in the East already a position second only to that of England, and should the European nations succeed in their plans of final interference in China, the United States, as the offensive arm of the coalition, might be called upon for prompt action of the most aggressive sort.

At the same time, after all has been said, it must be admitted that the United States is as yet only a potential factor in the international situation. Unless further aggression should be attempted in the Orient, or it should become necessary or expedient to change the nominal control over Mexico and Central America to actual possession, the United States will take no important share in hostilities, but will confine her efforts to the exceedingly important work, both to her allies and to herself, of keeping open the Atlantic highway and of protecting the merchant marine of England. Nor need one underestimate the importance of this task, for, should she fail to do her share, destruction might result for all concerned.

CHAPTER XI

FIRST DEFEATS

THE failure of their designs in South Africa and in South America turned German eyes to the northern part of the former continent, to the great dominion which the French possessed in Morocco. The strategic value of Morocco was undeniable, for it flanked the whole southern shore of the Mediterranean at the entrance opposite Gibraltar and extended far down the African coast. Together with Algeria and Tunis, it practically gave the French the whole of Africa east of the Libyan Desert, north of the Congo and of the Sahara Desert. Of this vast domain Morocco proper is one of the richest and most valuable parts. It is larger in area than Germany. Its exports and imports are considerable, each amounting to about fifteen million dollars annually. The climate is temperate, the soil fertile and varied, rich in minerals, and capable of almost indefinite development; the sparse population, amounting only to about five millions of people, most of them too barbarous and indolent either to use their country themselves or to oppose its use by some one else, would afford Germany an admirable field for colonization and the development of a market. As has already been said, the Germans had attempted to rouse the natives against the French, and, more especially in the southern part of Morocco, had attained conspicuous success. The actual outbreak, however, resulting from their influence was crushed with exceeding dispatch by the French, and the Germans began to be aware that the peaceful penetration of Morocco with French consent was more than improbable. In the summer of 1911, therefore, the Germans ventured upon a decisive step, and sent the warship Panther to anchor in the port of Agadir with the clear intention of interfering somehow in the state of affairs in Morocco. The port chosen for this demonstration seemed, despite rather conflicting testimony, to possess great possibilities as a naval station; the hinterland was reputed to be exceedingly rich in minerals; the river, which enters the sea at this point, was of considerable size and drained a very fertile district. Furthermore, Agadir was far enough removed from Fez and the seat of French authority to make it possible for the Germans to hold it without rousing too much apprehension in the minds of the French of clashes in the future. The excuse for the German interference officially put

forward — the protection of the Europeans at
Agadir — was an obvious pretext too slim to deceive any one. The number of Europeans in that
part of Morocco was exceedingly few, and they
were in absolutely no danger. The really logical
ground which Germany took was that she could
not recognize the validity of an agreement, permitting the French and English to monopolize
Morocco, to which she had not been a party. She
denied, in fact, the right of other European nations
to make with each other contracts and agreements,
concerning the disposition of the world in general,
which should be binding upon any but themselves.
She demanded, therefore, a new agreement which
should recognize her obvious interests and to
which she should be a party. As a possible equivalent, in case England and France should be unwilling to make such dispositions in Morocco as
her interests made desirable, she demanded the
cession to her by France of a district adjoining the
small territory she already possessed at Kamerun.
This district was a part of French Congo, the
southernmost part near and its value
area all proba-

which Belgium obtained access to her great domain in the Congo valley. The strategic value of the spot was as undeniable as its commercial importance. Perhaps Germany might succeed in cutting off the Belgians from the sea and compel them either to pay tolls or cede a portion of their estate in order to regain access to it.

The movement upon Morocco had a secret purpose quite as important as any other of its varied aspects. The Germans had long known of the existence of a secret understanding between England and France, but they had not been able to discover its exact terms, and it was of the utmost consequence for them to know whether or not the arrangement was solely defensive and applied to aggressive movements against either country in Europe, whether the agreement promised either country the other's assistance in case either should take the offensive, or whether it extended as an offensive and d̶e̶f̶e̶n̶sive alliance to the protection of both Fre̶n̶c̶h̶ ̶a̶n̶d English interests in every part of the wo̶r̶l̶d̶.̶ ̶T̶o̶ ̶d̶iscover, therefore, its precise limitati̶o̶n̶s̶ ̶t̶h̶e̶ ̶G̶e̶r̶m̶ans proposed to raise an issue wi̶t̶h̶ ̶F̶r̶a̶n̶c̶e̶.̶ ̶I̶f̶ ̶t̶h̶e̶y̶ ̶d̶i̶d̶ forward — the protection of the Europeans at Agadir — was an obvious pretext too slim to deceive any one. The number of Europeans in that part of Morocco was exceedingly few, and they were in absolutely no danger. The really logical ground which Germany took was that she could not recognize the validity of an agreement, permitting the French and English to monopolize Morocco, to which she had not been a party. She denied, in fact, the right of other European nations to make with each other contracts and agreements, concerning the disposition of the world in general, which should be binding upon any but themselves. She demanded, therefore, a new agreement which should recognize her obvious interests and to which she should be a party. As a possible equivalent, in case England and France should be unwilling to make such dispositions in Morocco as her interests made desirable, she demanded the cession to her by France of a district adjoining the small territory she already possessed at Kamerun. This district was a part of the French Congo, the southernmost part nearest the river, and its value far exceeded its area. In fact, it did in all probability equal in actual value at the moment the whole German colonial empire. In addition, it flanked the Congo, and also was situated adjacent to the little strip of territory along the river by which Belgium obtained access to her great domain in the Congo valley. The strategic value of the spot was as undeniable as its commercial importance. Perhaps Germany might succeed in cutting off the Belgians from the sea and compel them either to pay tolls or cede a portion of their estate in order to regain access to it.

The movement upon Morocco had a secret purpose quite as important as any other of its varied aspects. The Germans had long known of the existence of a secret understanding between England and France, but they had not been able to discover its exact terms, and it was of the utmost consequence for them to know whether or not the arrangement was solely defensive and applied to aggressive movements against either country in Europe, whether the agreement promised either country the other's assistance in case either should take the offensive, or whether it extended as an offensive and defensive alliance to the protection of both French and English interests in every part of the world. To discover, therefore, its precise limitations, the Germans proposed to raise an issue with France, whom they did not fear, which would promptly bring to the fore the question whether England should aid France in obtaining a decision favorable to her upon an issue in which England had no direct interest. Whatever

160

happened, the Germans could scarcely fail to obtain some valuable indications of the strength and extent of the Anglo-French Entente, and might even succeed in compelling one or the other of them publicly to acknowledge its existence and perhaps its terms. There was, therefore, much that Germany might gain from this aggressive movement at Agadir, and she did not seem to be greatly in danger of losing anything.

The event was eminently successful in drawing from England and France an acknowledgment of their hitherto secret understanding and an explicit statement of its extent. The English evidently considered that it amply covered the present case, which made clear to the Germans that the arrangement was by no means purely defensive, and that it certainly did not confine itself to encroachments upon the contracting countries in northern Europe, — information of the utmost importance. Supported thus by England and by the enthusiasm of the French people, the French Ministry forced the issue upon Germany and practically presented to the latter the alternative of receding from her demands or of undertaking war. In Germany the popular feeling in favor of war ran high, and even the best and coolest advisers of the Emperor seem to have counseled the undertaking of at least a demonstration in force upon the

French frontier, more, perhaps, with the notion of discovering the possible rapidity with which the French army could be mobilized than with any intention of fighting. Whether the Imperial advisers merely intended to prepare for all eventualities or were willing to yield to popular and military pressure and declare war, the Government certainly attempted to procure in Berlin the ready money necessary to finance the mobilization of the army. There then became evident the fact which probably astonished the Germans as much as it did every one else in the world outside of the few men in London and Paris who were responsible for it. It seems that German business was being transacted upon capital borrowed abroad, and that the German merchants had so extended their borrowing operations that more than ninety per cent of the current business transactions depended upon call loans or time loans secured in London and Paris. The moment the international situation became tense, a concerted movement was undertaken by the few men who controlled financial movements in those capitals for the recall of these loans. The result was as astonishing and as disastrous as it was intended to be. The ready cash in Germany was promptly moved out of the country, and many merchants found themselves compelled to sell securities to meet their pressing obligations. Not only, therefore, was the German nation for the moment seriously strained for gold, but the sale of securities was so considerable as to assume the proportions of a financial panic. The banks in Germany were on the verge of being compelled to suspend specie payments and were many of them almost bankrupt. There was no money to be had in Germany with which to begin the war. The Government, with unheard-of effrontery, appealed for loans to the great French and English banking houses, depending obviously upon the bankers' greed being stronger than their patriotism. The financial kings promptly informed the Emperor that they would be only too glad to furnish him such sums as he might require in exchange for proper securities and an engagement in his own handwriting not to use the loan for military purposes. The latter condition being obviously out of the question, the Emperor appealed to the American financiers and received from them a reply substantially the same. Thus unexpectedly was revealed the real financial strength of England and France and the value of the alliance with the United States. Germany had been defeated, for her enemies had it in their power to prevent her even from taking the field. Surely no defeat could have been more crushing or more humiliating.

163

The Germans made the best possible out of a bad business. They secured after long negotiations the addition of some territory to Kamerun, but they were compelled to agree to the French control of Morocco, to recognize, moreover, a control far more considerable and exclusive than before and which placed in the hands of France much more authority in administration. Subsequently, France came to terms with Spain, who had shown a good deal of uneasiness in regard to the changed conditions in Morocco, and whose Premier had officially made statements, regarding the determination of Spain to protect her interests in Africa, which were little short of defiance. That Spain was animated in this by direct suggestions from Berlin seemed eminently probable, and, even if it were not so, and she was acting purely upon her own initiative and in her own interests, it was not expedient to allow her to continue dissatisfied at this juncture. France and England, therefore, took pains thoroughly to pacify the Spaniard.

The victory in Morocco, the clear evidence that Germany's financial situation made war impossible for the moment, suggested to the Triple Entente the expediency of action in Persia, where matters were progressing in a direction favorable to Germany's designs, whether or not they were the result of her suggestion. The strategic position of Persia is of great significance. Her territory marches with the boundaries of Asia Minor and flanks the Baghdad Railway and the rich district of the Tigris and Euphrates upon which England has long had designs. It controls the northern coast of the Persian Gulf, the coast road to India, the most important harbors, and, from a military point of view, is absolutely essential to the safety of the English in India. On the other hand, the roads to the Black and Caspian Seas from India, the Persian Gulf, and southwestern Asia all pass through Persia, whose condition becomes therefore a matter of the utmost consequence to Russia. The railway has not yet penetrated this section of the world, and the old caravan routes are still of great commercial value. It is obvious that Persia is of vital importance to England and to Russia, neither of whom is willing to allow the other exclusive possession, and neither of whom can permit that territory to fall into the hands of people unwilling to recognize their interests. While less dangerous than possession by Germany, the creation in Persia of an independent state, with an efficient centralized government maintained by Persians in the interests of Persia, proclaiming as its chief *raison d'être* the exclusion of foreigners and the emancipation of Persia at the earliest possible moment from the financial shackles binding her to England and Russia, would be, from every point of view, quite as objectionable to the latter nations as any contingency they could imagine. The Shah had been continued upon the throne, the new constitution accepted by them because they had not expected the new government to be very different from the old; but the ability of Mr. Shuster, the Treasurer, the integrity and energy of his assistants, their evident intention to administer the state solely in the interests of Persia, and, above all, the enthusiastic response from the Persians, proved both to the English and the Russians that a state was in process of formation whose strength was growing daily and whose determination to accede to no more demands from them grew firmer month by month. Such a Persia might effectively stand in the way of their important interests. Moreover, neither of them considered the alternative for Persia to lie between her practical ownership by some European nation and her actual independence. The English feared, with probably good reason, that their recognition of the new state, followed by the withdrawal of their representatives, publicly or secretly, would be simply the signal for the absorption of Persia and the complete destruction of the new govern-

ment by Russia or by Germany. The same apprehensions were felt at St. Petersburg. Both Russia
and England, therefore, agreed that, from the
point of view of Persia herself, it would be better
in the long run for them to retain possession than
to permit the longer continuance of a state of
affairs, which might, in a few years, make Persia
the battle-ground of the two coalitions, with
results to the Persians which could easily be
imagined. Naturally, they did not expect the
Persians to accept this view of the situation, and
realized that the use of force would be indispensable.

A *casus belli* was easily found and could have
been as easily created. Every step taken by the
new Persian government was a tacit, if not an
open, nullification of the treaty relations in existence between Persia and the two countries. Mr.
Shuster and his administrators, and, in the main,
the more efficient and able of the Persians, were
ejected from office, and the old, inefficient, corrupt administration was restored, in fact if not
in name. The result upon politics in the Near
East was a defeat for Germany. As in the case
of Morocco, her interference resulted only in
strengthening the hold her enemies already possessed. Certainly, for the moment at any rate,
the Baghdad Railway was outflanked and the

possible extension of the German commercial route to the rich markets of the East was rendered for the time being highly improbable. Until some considerable change takes place, the commercial value of the Baghdad Railway will be confined to the possibility of developing the district of Asia Minor which it traverses.

The danger of ferment in Egypt among the native population and the military weakness of the English in that country did not escape the Ministry in London. Accordingly they sent to Egypt England's ablest soldier, Lord Kitchener. His mission was to improve the military dispositions of the force already available and the preparation of adequate plans for efficient defense. For the nonce, however, his important work was confined to the counteracting of the effects produced in the natives' minds by the German agents. To the educated and the officials, he was to make clear the undoubted fact that for them the alternative was, not the continuance of the present nominal relations between them and England, which left in their own hands a very extensive authority in local affairs, or their complete independence from interference by any one, but between the continuance of the *status quo* and their annexation by some member of the Triple Alliance, who would be forced by the exigencies of military occupation, or by the necessities of the defense, to impose upon Egypt a good deal severer a *régime* than the English ever intended to create. For them to continue schemes for the expulsion of the English would simply mean that they were exposing themselves to the tender mercies of the Triple Alliance. The strategic position of Egypt, the extraordinary fertility of the Nile Valley and its great exports of cotton and grain, the existence of the Suez Canal, all made it impossible for Egypt to be governed solely in the interest of the Egyptians. The rest of the world was too intimately affected by conditions in Egypt to permit the Egyptians to disregard their claims. That such circumstances as these would mean nothing to the bulk of the population was only too apparent. Lord Kitchener, therefore, inaugurated a series of enlightened judicial and agricultural reforms, intended to relieve the pressure of the Government upon the people themselves, and thus in an exceedingly practical manner remove the only possible grievances which would appear vital to the great bulk of the population. According to apparently trustworthy reports, he has succeeded to a remarkable degree in rousing the enthusiasm of the fellaheen for English rule. He has certainly endeared himself to the population, and secured over them a personal influence which may conceivably be a factor of importance at no distant date in the destinies of empire.

Another great diplomatic victory seems to have been won by the English in India. The approaching coronation of George V as Emperor of India made possible the assemblage at Delhi of all the potentates of India and allied states. Their conjunction at one moment might conceivably result in the completion of plans for concerted revolt against the English, if any such were on foot, whether due to German, Russian, or native influence, but their presence might also be utilized for the execution of a diplomatic *coup* of the very first consequence. It would depend, however, for its success upon the presence of the King. No English sovereign had ever set foot in India, and it was considered that the King would certainly expose himself to assassination by undertaking to be crowned in person at the approaching Durbar at Christmas, 1911. At the same time, unless the information regarding the state of affairs in India was entirely wrong, the danger of an attack would be confined solely to his being shot or destroyed by a bomb from the crowd during some public ceremony. The stake for which to play was undoubtedly great, but the Ministers were not in favor of the King's assuming the necessary risks.

George, however, displayed a wholly admirable courage and an unexpected firmness of decision by insisting upon undertaking the difficult task. His presence in India, his coronation and safe return would be the most dramatic and conclusive possible refutation of the tales so rife in Europe about the disloyalty of the Hindus and the precarious condition of England in India. The event more than justified the expectations. The King rode through the streets as he might have ridden through London; he sat alone with the Queen upon a great throne, fully exposed to thousands of people; he sat again alone with the Queen, with no guards in sight, upon a parapet near the road down which passed a great stream of Hindus of all conditions. The opportunities for his assassination were many. More than once the rumor spread that he had been killed. The tension during his stay was certainly extreme. But nothing happened. The moral effect of the Durbar in India and in Europe was great.

The real purpose, however, of the King's presence in India was far otherwise than the mere demonstration that he could be there for some weeks without being shot. He undertook the extremely difficult task of explaining by word of mouth to the Indian potentates the intricacies of the international situation and their practical

relation to India. Coming from him by word of
mouth such representations could not fail to have
weight. They would certainly have never been
believed had the rulers learned them from any
subordinate, however exalted in station. Besides,
there can be little question that the King con-
fided to them many things which it is not considered wise that most men should know. Undoubtedly, he explained to them the fact that the
alternative for the Hindus, as it is for the Egyptians and the Persians, is not actual independence from English rule, but a choice between the
rule of England, Russia, or Germany. He can
have had no great difficulty in demonstrating
the honesty and excellence of English administration, and the great moderation of the English
Government in never spending outside India a
penny of the money collected in India; that the
only benefit England has ever received directly
has been the legitimate profits of trade; that
Russia or Germany would offer more favorable
terms is not likely; that the English were more
than ready to meet the reasonable demands of
the Hindus halfway; and that the English would
consider reasonable anything which did not involve the loss of their trading monopoly or the
weakening of the defensive strength of India
against Russia and Germany. Naturally, these

are purely conjectures of what the King must have said. The results are also purely conjectural, but certainly any statement at all of the realities of the situation cannot fail to have been convincing. It is hard for an impartial observer to see any possible advantage to the Hindu of an exchange of rulers.

The year 1911, therefore, was one of pretty conspicuous success in all directions for England and France. Everywhere they seemed to have successfully met Germany, and everywhere to have disproved her prophecy that their colonial empires would fall to pieces of their own weight. However real the weakness might be, however possible the success of Germany's schemes, the weakness certainly was not apparent, and the probability of Germany's success did not seem immediate.

CHAPTER XII

THE English and the French were by no means satisfied with the character of the measures which they had undertaken for thwarting the schemes of the Triple Alliance.[1] Indeed, they had merely succeeded in holding their own, had in no sense placed any barrier in the way of the execution of Pan-Germanism, nor could they do so by such measures as they had previously espoused. Something structural was necessary, basic, fundamental in character, going to the root of the German scheme, which they very well realized was not in the least touched by their successes in Persia and Morocco. It was clear that Italy was for many reasons the least ardent member of the Triple Alliance and had the least to gain from the success of Pan-Germanism. Her hatred of Austria was still vigorous, and the necessary possession by Austria of the Balkans, her inevitable growth in naval power, the obvious advantage to the coalition of her securing control of the Adriatic

[1] Individual sentences in chapters XII and XIII and the concluding paragraphs of chapter XIII have been taken from the author's article in the *Forum* for December, 1912.

174

and the Ægean, could not fail to rouse in the minds of the Italians certain eminently natural apprehensions. To strengthen Austria along the Illyrian coast meant to increase her strength in that very quarter least acceptable to Italy,[1] for Trieste could not fail to become a rival of Venice, and the increase of Austrian power in the Adriatic would necessarily interfere with Italy's ambitions to control the whole commerce of that sea. Nor was control of the Adriatic less essential to her as an outlet for the commerce of the Po Valley than it was for Austria. To say that Italy could ship her goods to the western seaports along the Mediterranean, could easily be met by saying that Austria could also ship her goods by rail wherever she wished. Moreover, Italy had been steadily penetrating the eastern shores of the Adriatic by the familiar peaceful methods of loans and investments, and had already large interests in Albania, Scutari, and Epirus, whose proximity to Italy made her interest in them natural. Nor could the fact that the present Queen of Italy is a Montenegrin princess fail to rouse concern at Rome for the future of that

[1] "Our Eastern frontiers, I said [Crispi speaking to Bismarck], are extremely exposed, and should Austria's position on the Adriatic be strengthened, we should be held as in a vice, and our safety would be threatened." Dispatch from Crispi to the King of Italy, 1877. *Memoirs of Francesco Crispi*, II, 64. London, 1912.

England and France, after studying carefully
the situation in the Mediterranean, concluded
from the fact of Italy's continued alliance with
Germany and Austria and the certainty that
Austria would claim, as her share of the plunder,
the Balkans and the eastern coast of the Adriatic,
that Italy's part could be nothing less, and was
not improbably nothing more, than Tripoli. In
any case, whatever she was promised, she would
be compelled to wait for until the success of a
scheme whose execution was barely begun and
which might not succeed at all. They, therefore,
approached Italy, offered to insure her possession
of Tripoli at once without fighting, without expense, and without delay; if she should put forward some technical *casus belli* and should make a
vigorous show of force in Tripoli, she could then
be accorded possession by a treaty with the Turk,
whose terms the three conspirators would arrange
to their mutual satisfaction. Incidentally they
would test the efficiency of the new Turkish army.
She would, of course, in return desert the Triple
Alliance, and form an alliance with them, whose
strength would secure them all possession of everything they desired in the Mediterranean for some
decades. The Italian navy added to the French
navy would so far preponderate over the Austrian and Turkish fleets that the English Medi-

terranean squadron could be practically with-
drawn. Thus, without at all endangering the
security of its control of the Mediterranean, the
new alliance could make so immediate and considerable an increase of strength to its naval forces
in the English Channel as to outnumber the German fleet for a good many years to come. Italy's
position flanking the Adriatic would make Austria's control of that sea improbable; the strength
of the new alliance would make exceedingly difficult any further accessions of territory by Austria
in the Balkans; and thus Italy would be secure.
By rendering impossible the effective use of the
Ægean by Austria, the possibility of an attack by
the latter's fleet from the rear of Malta upon the
English lines of communication with Egypt and
India, and upon the Italian lines of communication with her new possession, would be eliminated;
Sicily and Sardinia would strengthen the lines of
advance already centering at Malta and would
make the position of the allies in the western Mediterranean literally impregnable. With Tripoli in
Italy's hands, even the success of Germany and
Austria in creating their proposed confederation,
stretching from the North Sea to the Persian Gulf,
would not be serious. Of course, while the Turk
retained even nominal control of Tripoli, the fact
that he was only too obviously falling deeper and

an annual deficit, and was particularly bitter because of the former expectation that possession of the new province would in one way or another lighten the financial burdens of the mother country. Actual conquest by the sword would certainly so embitter the natives as to make the government of Tripoli expensive and difficult for years to come. The Italians, in short, had been placed by their friends in a very real dilemma, from which their friends were unable to extricate them and from which, indeed, it was doubtful whether the Italians could successfully extricate themselves without paying a price greater than they were able to afford.

Under such circumstances, with such calamities expected and such hopes unfulfilled, the Italians received from the Wilhelmstrasse whispered communications of cheering import. If Italy would return to the Triple Alliance, pointed out the Germans, her old friends would be able to secure for her without cost or difficulty the possession of Tripoli, and in time a great deal more. Indeed, said the Germans, the present dilemma in which Italy found herself proved conclusively the truth of the German assertions regarding the weakness of England and France. It proved no less astounding a proposition than that the English control of the Mediterranean was a sham.

Italy, in fact, if she would return to the Triple Alliance, might practically reverse the situation in the Mediterranean and bring Tripoli with her for nothing; the strategic positions on which England and France had based their defense of the Mediterranean would be vastly weakened, if not destroyed; the naval force, which they had believed virtually preponderant, would be reduced to a bare equality which would make offensive movements impossible and render the success of defensive movements problematical; not a lira need be spent, not a life sacrificed to make the conquest of the Mediterranean an eminently feasible operation and to strike a more deadly blow at English naval supremacy than it had suffered since the Seven Years' War. Such substantial and probable achievements would have been themselves considered the worthy fruits of a hard-fought and costly war, and here they could actually be had for nothing!

The English had already changed their naval arrangements in the Mediterranean, counting upon the presence of the Italians to neutralize the Austrian navy for the time being, and the French had not yet executed their part of the agreement by concentrating their fleet in the Mediterranean. For the moment, the Italian and Austrian fleets, while not strong enough to take tary measure but would be permanent. So confident of success were the Italians. The existence of the new naval base in Tripoli, the possession of the strategic points of the eastern Mediterranean by a member of the Triple Alliance, snatched from England the entire control of the eastern Mediterranean and threw her back upon Malta, whose position was instantly changed from that of the central position of England's defensive chain to that of an outpost. Italy's change of front of course promptly suspended active hostilities between herself and Turkey, though the Turk obstinately refused to remove the new Turkish army from Tripoli. After all, from the point of view of the Alliance, this was not altogether regrettable, for it gave a tinge of reality to the military dispositions Italy proceeded to make with promptitude on the coast and along the caravan lines leading into Egypt.

CHAPTER XIII

MEANWHILE, the Triple Alliance, thus reunited, proceeded with the complementary details of the scheme. The German, Austrian, and Italian naval programmes were at once enlarged, the proposed German fleet was made nearly equal in number to the proposed English Channel squadron and the Austro-Italian fleet was already the equal of the entire French battle fleet; an increased activity of building, therefore, was expected to give the allies in a couple of years something like equality, if not actual superiority, both in the Mediterranean and in the German Ocean. Indeed, the situation had been so changed as to make it difficult for England and France to meet the crisis merely by a rearrangement of the existing forces. The chief reason for their desire to detach Italy from the Triple Alliance was interpreted in Berlin to be their realization that they had practically reached the limit of their resources and could no longer continue to build at the same rate as before. To strengthen the Mediterranean fleet by an alliance with Italy would have enabled them to increase the Channel squadron without additional expense. The *coup d'état* in the Mediterranean changed the whole naval situation by strengthening the position of the Triple Alliance in that sea, and rendered inadequate the previous dispositions of England and France. A large fleet, more naval stations, and very different equipment of certain stations would be necessary satisfactorily to meet the crisis. To strengthen the fleet in the Mediterranean meant the weakening of the English fleet in the Atlantic and the considerable reduction of the number of vessels which Germany must build to change England's old predominance into something like equality. This, then, was the moment for which the allies had been waiting. There was now a fair chance of their creating within a reasonable time enough ships to compass that equality of armament which England had always declared would be so fatal to her welfare. The military dispositions of the allies, the facilities for prompt mobilization, the railway facilities along the Belgian and French and Russian frontiers, were all considered with a view to their adequacy for actual war. The work on the Baghdad Railway was pushed with the utmost energy; the little band of able men, whom Germany had so long kept in Constantinople, busied in reconstructing Turkey, were recalled to

Europe. The German Emperor began, with his usual energy, a round of visits to all the sovereigns of whom anything was expected or from whom anything was feared. To them all he explained, no doubt, the great advantage just secured and made, by word of mouth, promises, assurances, and explanations, which could not have been entrusted to subordinates. Unquestionably, the energy of Wilhelm II, his persuasive powers, and his faith in this gigantic scheme have been of vital importance in securing the coöperation of Germany's present allies and in bringing their plans to their present state of completion.

The English and French, astonished and alarmed at the unexpected turn of affairs, strained every nerve to meet it by preparations which should be more than adequate for any emergency. Both have felt, however, that to avow publicly the extent of the danger would produce an unfavorable effect on English and French public opinion, either by sapping popular confidence in the national strength, or, more probably, by causing a demand for instant war which it would be difficult to resist. In some way, without declaring immediate a danger which may after all be merely contingent, the people must be made to realize that a crisis is at hand of so serious a nature that it can be adequately met only by the immediate adop-

tion of the most extensive naval and military preparations either nation has yet undertaken. So
extensive are the plans, so long is the time which
will be required for their completion, so great will
be the financial burden imposed upon the people,
that the average individual, in nations which have
systematically encouraged him to have opinions
upon matters of national import, is more than
likely to deem such plans justifiable only to avert
an impending crisis, in which the very national
existence would be at stake, and to demand at
once financial sacrifices which he is likely to
approve only when the danger is exceedingly tangible. The present condition, therefore, which the
English and French Governments find it most
difficult to meet, is the fact that the time and
expense for what they believe to be the necessary
preparations are in themselves proof to the average man that the emergency is contingent rather
than immediate. They are hampered, as the Germans have always claimed they would be under
such circumstances, by the difficulty of convincing
the ordinary individual of the expediency of spending as much money in order to postpone or avert
a war as would seem to him necessary to prosecute
it. To tell the public that the war is already going
on, that it is being fought with every variety of
weapon, except armies and navies, that England

is really in danger, and at the same time to prove to him that the English navy largely outnumbers the navies of the Triple Alliance, is simply to demonstrate the expediency of fighting now before the preparations of the Triple Alliance already announced destroy England's superiority.

In England, too, the position of parties in the House of Commons is actually hampering the Government in its preparations to meet the crisis, as the Germans have always claimed it would. The Liberals, who are nominally in power, are absolutely dependent upon the support of the Irish Nationalists and of the Laborites. The former group are exceedingly anxious to secure the final passage into law, without substantial amendment, of the Home Rule Bill just passed by the House of Commons. The most important clause of that bill provides for the payment out of the Imperial Treasury to the new Irish Government of a subsidy annually sufficient in amount to pay for the construction of two or more battleships. The Irish Budget has so long shown an annual deficit, and it has so long been evident that the Irish people are paying more taxes than they can really afford, that the advocates of Home Rule know perfectly well that, without substantial assistance from England, Home Rule is impossible. The Irish people are incapable of paying their own bills. But to secure such a subsidy at the moment of moments when English naval supremacy is more nearly in danger than at any time in the last two centuries, when that amount of money annually expended might suffice to maintain England's supremacy, is, as they well know, exceedingly questionable. The pressure of this very situation, however, the absolute necessity which English statesmen feel for directing the affairs of the Empire in accordance with their own conception of its needs and without interference from the Irish Nationalists, convinces the latter that they have the best chance they have ever had to extort Home Rule from England even on these terms.

They have pointed out to the disconsolate Ministry the fact that they can hamper England's utilization of the resources she now possesses to an extent which might be fatal, and that the Ministry which is now in power can remain in power only so long as they are willing, and, concomitantly, that the Ministry which will replace it can remain in power only on the same terms. The very fact that the alternative lies between using what England has and the increase of its force is to them the most important weapon in their arsenal. England must in self-defense come to terms with them. The Labor members are opposed to war on any terms. They have not scrupled publicly to declare that they owned nothing in England which the conquest of England by Germany could possibly take away from them, neither land, nor houses, nor wealth. They have the clothes on their backs; they are promised, so long as they work, enough food to keep them alive. This, they declare scornfully, is the sum total of their interest in the maintenance of the British Empire. Could the Germans offer them less? Whether because the Irish and the Laborites do not believe the danger great, or because they are determined to achieve their own objects, whatever the cost to England, is not clear; but the fact is certain that they have effectively prevented the adoption in the House of Commons of as large an increase of the naval appropriations as the Ministry desired to make, and have stoutly refused to approve conscription in any form.

Knowing this, the Germans could not fail to consider a confession of weakness Mr. Churchill's public promise to decrease the English naval programme in proportion to any decrease in German plans, and his hint that England would be willing formally to guarantee the immunity of the Austrian seacoast from attack if the plans for the increase of the Austrian navy should be abandoned; his scarcely veiled threat, to surpass in number any increase they might attempt to make, they greeted with open derision. They believed that they had powerful allies in the English Ministry and in the English House of Commons, and, so confident were they that these allies would prevent him from executing his threat, that they announced a very substantial increase in the German and Austrian naval estimates. Such action was tantamount to a direct challenge to fulfill his threat, and the amazing fact is that he could not do it. The Laborites and the Home Rulers flatly refused to sanction Mr. Churchill's measures; they flatly declared they would oppose similar measures introduced by the opposite party, in case the Ministry should resign; and compelled the adoption of a compromise measure providing for so small an increase that, by the public admission of the First Lord of the Admiralty, Germany will have within two years twenty-nine ships in the North Sea to England's thirty-three. The Opposition both in the Commons and in the Lords, as well as the foremost naval and military authorities, are insisting in the frankest language that the Supplementary Estimates are utterly inadequate. Naturally, the knowledge of these facts has not diminished the confidence felt at Berlin, Vienna, and Rome, and it has so obviously weakened confidence at Paris, that some of the influential journals have actually begun to question the value of England's support should she lose, not her control of the Channel by actual fighting, but her naval preponderance. Indeed, the contrast is sufficiently striking between the prompt passage of a considerable Supplementary Estimate without dissent by a Reichstag utterly hostile to the administration, and the grudging passage of so slight an increase by the English House of Commons where the existing Ministry nominally controlled so powerful a majority as to have overridden even strenuous opposition to other measures. The Ministry has done what it could to counteract these doubts by secret promises and assurances. The naval dispositions in the Mediterranean have been carefully examined; conferences held between the French and the English authorities; the English and French naval boards went over the ground in person in the summer of 1912, and no doubt arrived at important conclusions. Lord Kitchener's success in Egypt, the results of the King's visit to India, continued success in Persia, also gave the Triple Entente confidence.

The most encouraging aspect of the situation has been the prompt and enthusiastic response of the English self-governing colonies to the appeal of the mother country for assistance. Several have adopted naval programmes; their ships are already under construction; they have promised to add their vessels to the English navy and to leave their direction entirely in the hands of the Admiralty in London. The Canadian Ministry has asked the Parliament to appropriate money for three first-class battleships, and will in all probability succeed in carrying the measure. This aid is so considerable in amount as to be of really substantial importance.

The English also have reorganized the entire administration of their fleet, both for offense and defense; they have created a school for the training in strategy of officers; and have instituted in addition a special board of experts, in whose hands will be placed, in time of action, the direction of operations.

France has officially adopted the Two Power Standard in the Mediterranean, which is understood to mean that she will create and maintain a fleet sufficiently numerous easily to outweigh the combined Italian and Austrian navies. Spain's assistance or, perhaps, neutrality the allies have bought with concessions in Morocco. Russia, frightened at the prospect of the loss of the position in the Baltic she now possesses, has signed a naval convention with France, which pledges her to a rapid and really considerable

increase of her Baltic fleet and the creation of a new naval base almost on the Prussian frontier. The existence of a really powerful Russian fleet in the Baltic might interfere vitally with the further execution of Germany's present plans. Berlin and all North Germany would be exposed to its attack; the Kiel Canal might be destroyed; the rear of the Atlantic squadron would be exposed to its operations; and its strength might be sufficient to compel the division of the German North Sea fleet, an eventuality which would so weaken the forces available for an offensive war as to postpone its date by years, if it did not make its outcome so uncertain as to prevent it altogether.

But the most significant movement is the project for the Trans-Persian Railway which England, France, and Russia have adopted. The line is to run southeast from Teheran to Bushire in the English zone of influence and to follow the coast of the Persian Gulf to Karachi. Unquestionably, a Russian army arriving in India by that route would turn the flank of Quetta and render useless all the fortifications and dispositions yet made to keep Russia out of India. For England to consent to it is to abandon the policy of isolating India from Europe by preventing the establishment of easy communication by land. Should

Russia attack from Herat and from the new railroad line at the same moment, nothing could
prevent the overwhelming of the English army.
Russia has three quarters of a million men en-
rolled in her army who live within two thousand
miles of the Indian frontier. They may not be
highly trained, but they will certainly outnumber
the English army ten to one, and the combined
native and English troops four to one. Lord
Curzon voices the convictions of many Anglo-
Indians when he declares that the construction
of the Trans-Persian Railway is the death-knell
of the British power in India. It means, further,
the admission of Russia to the rich marts of India,
and a recognition of her right to share directly
in that trade; and whatever its effect may be on
English retention of the sovereignty in India, it
will at once end England's practical monopoly
of Indian trade. To the British merchant and
manufacturer there would seem to be little left
worth struggling for, if that is renounced.

Such, however, are not the purposes of that
railway, and such will not necessarily be the results
of its construction. The project is based upon the
absolute necessity for an English military road
to India in case Germany and her allies succeed
in securing actual control of the Mediterranean.
The new road would prevent the use by Germany

of the Baghdad Railway and the Persian Gulf as an approach to India. It would enable England, so long as her alliance with Russia lasted, to reinforce the Indian army far more rapidly than would be possible by way of the Panama Canal and the Pacific. In fact, should the Triple Alliance secure control of the Mediterranean, nothing short of some such road would enable England and Russia combined to place enough troops in India to prevent its immediate conquest by Germany. England wishes to keep it; Russia has always dreamed of possessing it; but both would rather see it in the hands of the other than allow Germany to get it. Such an increase of German power would at once endanger the very existence of England and the continued possession by Russia of any territories in the Baltic or in Poland. To the English Ministry, moreover, the danger of losing India because of the new railway's construction seems small beside the undeniable military value of the road as an offensive measure against Germany. The road will run mainly through British territory; it will follow the coast of the Persian Gulf, and therefore can always be controlled by an English fleet; nor will it put Russia nearer the Indian defenses than she is already; the lookouts at Herat can almost see a Russian railway station, and Herat is the key to

India, scarcely a fourth as far from the frontier and Quetta as Teheran is from Karachi. In fact, say the English military experts, Russia already possesses quite as favorable a position for an assault as the railway would afford her; but clearly she does not wish to use it, nor will she desire to do so as long as the assistance of England and France is necessary to prevent Germany from overrunning the Baltic.

The feasibility of a military road to India through Russia and Persia has been many times declared. The route through Turkestan, across the Caspian and up the Russian rivers, was one of the commonest roads followed by invasion after invasion from Asia; it was one of the recognized trade routes of Europe during the Middle Ages, and was well worn by the feet of merchants. Upon its existence, the English Muscovy Company depended, and from the trade grew wealthy. Until the construction of the Suez Canal, it was as practicable as any land route and more rapid, though more expensive and dangerous, than the voyage round the Cape of Good Hope. Through it Alexander invaded India, and no less a soldier than Napoleon himself conceived the idea of following the precise route the English and Russians propose to employ in case of need. Napoleon had the whole route carefully surveyed and measured, and his engineers reported its entire practicability.

In addition, if we suppose the existence of a general European war and an attempt by Germany on India at a time when England could spare neither men nor ships from European waters, the new railway would enable her to permit a sufficient Russian force to enter India to defeat the Germans without actually delivering into Russia's hands the keys of the Himalayas, Herat and Quetta. Should Russia after defeating Germany turn traitor, the English in India, with the possession of Quetta and the aid of the fleet set free by Germany's defeat, might still make a good fight. Should Germany decisively defeat the Channel fleet while her allies were overrunning the Mediterranean, the deluge would have already arrived, and India would be irretrievably lost, railway or no railway, and England would be glad to see a nation strengthened by the possession of India which might do battle with the all-conquering German. The Trans-Persian Railway is not necessarily desirable; it seems to the English merely the best of a number of extremely undesirable and regrettable expedients of which unfortunately one must be chosen. So a deputation of the members of the House of Commons and of London merchant princes visited Russia and formally sanctioned the commercial aspects of the military agreement. The incident shows conclusively how dependent England is upon her allies and how much trust she is forced to repose in them. It indicates with even greater certainty the English belief in the feasibility of the German plans for securing possession of the Mediterranean and Suez Canal.

CHAPTER XIV

THE great success of the war in Tripoli, as a method of extorting territory from the Turk and of preventing the interference of England and France with the execution of the plans for the rearrangement of the Mediterranean without the employment of actual force, promptly suggested to the diplomats and statesmen in Berlin and Vienna the prosecution of war in the Balkans. The Turk was unexpectedly reluctant to resign to Italy, even at the instigation of his new masters, the rich province of Tripoli. It seemed to the Young Turks the last straw, that, at just the moment when they were seeking to rouse in Turkey a national spirit, and to secure control of the government for a national party, whose policy should be based upon the interests of Turkey and not upon those of Europe, they should be forced at the very outset to consent to the dismemberment of Turkey as the condition of their longer continuance in power. It seemed to them, in fact, that, if they must yield in Tripoli, autonomy would never be a reality in Turkey, and the visions they had long cherished, and the material privations they had endured for the last decade or more, would be all rendered futile. The Triple Alliance obviously needed some lever with which to pry Tripoli from the clutches of the Young Turk without the necessity of actually taking it. It was, furthermore, highly essential that the Young Turk should not execute a *coup d'état* and desert them for the old alliance with England and France. That, above all, must not be risked. Some method must be found which would put pressure upon him without permitting him to desert and without allowing England or France an opportunity to interfere. The obvious method was war in the Balkans, where the military movements could be undertaken by the states, whose relations with the Turk were always tense, and whose private grievances were so familiar and so adequate in the eyes of Europe as fully to justify a resort to arms. The Turk would thus be between two fires. With war in Europe and war in Africa and only one army, he would be compelled to preserve Tripoli at the risk of defeat in Europe, or to renounce Tripoli and conclude peace with Italy on Italy's own terms, in order to insure the safety of his dominions in Europe. The moment also was most opportune for an attempt to rearrange affairs in the Balkans, and to attempt the realization of the Balkan Confederacy, on whose creation the final success of Pan-Germanism absolutely depended. The tense situation in Europe; the dangers to which the English and French were obviously exposed in the Mediterranean by the inability to use their previous naval dispositions for regaining control of the eastern Mediterranean; the time which must necessarily elapse before a force sufficient to regain that control could be assembled in the Mediterranean, all these factors made their actual interference improbable. The Germans calculated that, the odds being against England, she would not dare risk action. Therefore, with the probability of a free hand, the opportunity seemed ripe for the prosecution of the schemes for the reorganization of southeastern Europe.

The programme was practically made public by Austria, who advocated decentralization in Turkey along the lines already suggested, but never executed, in the Treaty of Berlin. The notion was to break up European Turkey by creating independent states in Albania and Macedonia and to make a new state out of the remains of Turkey in Europe. These three states, with the older communities of Rumania, Bulgaria, Servia, Montenegro, and perhaps Greece, should form a new confederation, governing the whole

of the district between the Austrian and Russian
frontiers and the Ægean and Mediterranean
seas.[1] Asia Minor would become the seat of the
old Turkish Empire and should be bound tightly
to Germany or Austria, and, if that were not
possible, to the new confederation, by bonds
which practically would compel the Turk to renounce control of policy and resources. In some
way or other, by commercial agreements, if no
more direct method was available, Austria was
to secure Saloniki as a naval base from which to
control the Ægean and the whole eastern Mediterranean, and either Austria or Italy was to
secure the remainder of the eastern shore of the
Adriatic. The allies calculated that a little show
of force by the Balkan States would put enough
pressure upon the Turks to compel the cession of
Tripoli, and might also drive the Young Turks
from power and reinstate the old bureaucracy,
whom Austria and Germany already owned body
and soul. Then the Treaty of Berlin could be
interpreted in such a manner as to enable the
allies to claim that the other Powers had already
given their consent to the new scheme of reorganization, would permit them to insist that no European Congress was necessary, and that the execu-

[1] The notion of a Balkan confederation supported by the Triple
Alliance seems to have originated in 1889. Crispi, *Memoirs*, ii, 384–
385.

tion of the Treaty ought completely to satisfy all parties. The irony of the situation would be that they would thus possess the Turk's own consent to his own destruction before they conquered him. When these arrangements were finished, and it seemed hardly doubtful but that they could be completed, Pan-Germanism would be practically a reality. There would be much yet to do, but formally it would have come into existence.

There were also vital reasons for attempting action in the fall of 1912. The death of the Emperor Franz Josef has been expected at any moment during the last few years and becomes more probable each month. Inasmuch as his death has been confidently expected to give the signal for a general revolt throughout the Dual Monarchy, it was highly essential to move before such a catastrophe deprived Austria of the possibility of action. Indeed, his death might force the allies to devote their time for some years to the reorganization of Austria-Hungary before they could proceed further with the scheme. Success in the Balkans and in Turkey, the actual creation of a Pan-Germanic chain, would not improbably so impress public opinion as to insure the continuance of the present arrangements and thwart the schemes of the irreconcilables. Should worst come to worst, a third monarchy could be created out of the

Croatian and Slavonic and Serbonian communities in southwestern Austria which would have the same relations to Austria as Hungary, would satisfy the most dangerous malcontents and enable the Empire to deal effectively with Bohemia and Galicia. Such an eventuality, however, raised many possible questions and would be certain to rouse suspicion in the Balkans. The adoption by England and Russia of the scheme for the Trans-Persian Railway, obviously a military road to circumvent the Baghdad Railway, to retain control of the Persian Gulf and render ineffectual the seizure of Suez, proved to the Germans that no time was to be lost, if the conquest of India, as the ultimate aim of the great confederation, was not to become impossible. The loss of India, Germany could not consider calmly, for the creation and maintenance of the Pan-German Confederation would compel her to hand over to her allies practically all the gains in the Mediterranean and in Europe, and her own share was to be India. The Panama Canal, moreover, another military road to the East, was nearing completion, would probably be practical as early as January, 1914, and its completion is expected to render the control of the Mediterranean and Red Sea infinitely less important to England than before. The risks of immediate action did not seem too great; the probable gains were undeniable; and the allies therefore decided upon action.

The Balkan States, who received intimations of the desirability of war from Berlin and Vienna, were astounded to receive, almost simultaneously, suggestions of the desirability of war with Turkey from London, Paris, and St. Petersburg. The Triple Entente had made up its mind that the moment was opportune for an attempt to erect a barrier in the way of Pan-Germanism which should not improbably postpone its execution at least a decade. Only in the Balkans could they hope in the long run successfully to oppose the Triple Alliance, nor could there be, from their point of view, a more favorable spot for opposition. The Balkan peoples had long hated Austria for racial and religious reasons, were determined, if possible, to win their own national independence, and, presenting, therefore, unusual difficulties to the statesmen seeking to amalgamate them with the Triple Alliance, furnished the latter's enemies the most favorable field in which to work. The strategic position of the Balkans, controlling all the roads between Europe and Asia Minor, controlling the Ægean and the Adriatic, was so necessary to Pan-Germanism, that no more deadly blow could possibly be dealt that scheme than the creation of a Balkan confederacy under the ægis of the Triple Entente, pledged to independence for the Balkan peoples of both coalitions. The stronger the confederation, the more independent, the greater obstacle it would be in the path of Pan-Germanism. The very qualities and resources, which would lead the Balkans to desire freedom from entangling alliances with the Triple Entente itself, would be the very qualities which would render improbable any agreement with the Triple Alliance, and would animate them with a patriotism and a determination to resist which could not fail to work for the benefit of the Triple Entente. For it is not necessary that the latter should itself control them. Its dispositions in the Mediterranean will be equally benefited if their possession by the Triple Alliance is rendered improbable. From the point of view of England and France, moreover, who necessarily distrust somewhat their ally, Russia, because of her ambitions in the Black Sea, the stronger the confederation, the more independent, the greater would be their own safety from possible treachery on the part of Russia.

At the same time both nations realized that the Tripolitan War had completely changed their own policies in regard to Turkey. Their objection to Russia at Constantinople had been based upon

the desire to exclude from the Mediterranean all
possible rivals; but the loss of Tripoli, the loss of
Turkey, both of which had fallen into the hands
of their enemies, and the fear of the creation of a
confederacy of states in the Balkans under German or Austrian protection, thoroughly disposed
of their objections to Russia's ownership of that
same territory. If they must have a rival in those
seas, a thousand times better that it should be
Russia than the Triple Alliance. Russia's Black
Sea fleet has still to be made powerful enough to
be able to interfere in the Mediterranean; she is so
dependent upon their assistance to preserve her
present position in northeastern Europe that she
is not likely to take action elsewhere which would
be contrary enough to their interests to cause a
rupture of the Entente. On the other hand, the
mere possession of the Balkans by Russia would
be as permanent a guarantee as could well be
imagined of the failure of Pan-Germanism for all
time, and would, more than any other one thing,
render Morocco, India, and even England itself
safe from aggression. In the Black Sea, Russia
could create, safe from interference, a fleet which
could issue forth from the Straits in time of need
and fall upon the rear of the Austro-Italian fleet
operating from the Adriatic or Tripoli. Should
Russia be able to secure possession of all the

Balkans, she would also control the Ægean and
the Adriatic, would occupy in Servia a post in
the rear of Hungary, highly dangerous to the
Dual Monarchy, from which an invasion, simultaneous with an attack through Galicia, could
hardly fail to have fatal consequences. Russia
in the Balkans, in other words, would promptly
compel Germany and Austria to take up the defensive and to do so under distinct disadvantages.
Once Russia occupied such a position, England
and France could promptly overrun the Mediterranean, take Trieste, conquer the Adriatic, isolate
Italy, compel her at the very least to cede Tripoli.
Thus they could secure a firmer hold upon the
Mediterranean than ever before. From Russia's
point of view, an independent confederation in
the Balkans, coupled to the right of freedom of
passage through the Straits and the permission
to create a fleet in the Black Sea, would be practically as advantageous a solution as she could
ask. Aside from the plains of the Lower Danube,
the Balkans themselves are of little value to her,
and so vitally threaten Austria that war could
hardly be avoided. Russia is more anxious to
open the Black Sea and to obtain naval control
than she is to force the issue with Austria at
present. An independent Balkan confederation
would protect the Straits from Austria, and would

in practice, whatever treaties and agreements might say, give her control.

Should the war succeed, the Turk could certainly be driven from Constantinople, and even if it were expedient to leave him there he might be compelled or induced to create a Khalifate in Egypt or Arabia to rule the Mohammedans in the English and French possessions. The latter are extremely desirous of quieting the religious ferment which has so hampered their actions on more than one occasion, by substituting for a religious head of the Mohammedans, held in the clutches of Germany, a religious head in their own control. They wish to remove the excuse for a Holy War, or, at any rate, to prevent the declaration of a Holy War by the Sultan in Constantinople which Mohammedans throughout the world would feel bound to recognize. Pan-Islam is a spectre terrifying to them in the extreme. Moreover, should the Germans achieve anything like further success in the reorganization, so-called, of southeastern Europe, it would become absolutely necessary for some member of the Triple Entente to take possession of Constantinople, to say the least, and, not improbably, to put an end to the nominal independence of Turkey. Such a blow at the Sultan would certainly be resented in India, Egypt, and Morocco, and the statesmen are ex-

tremely anxious either to remove the Sultan from
the danger zone or to shear him of his religious
headship.

The Balkan States scarcely believed in the
verity of these communications. The splendor
of the opportunity fairly dazzled their eyes. It
had long seemed to them that there was really a
chance to free themselves from the shackles of
both coalitions and of winning from the Turk,
without much difficulty, their freedom and that
of their compatriots in the Turkish Empire, so
long as the two coalitions did not actually support Turkey. Of that fact they were apprehensive.
While the Turk had been the Sick Man of Europe,
maintained by the Powers because of the incurable nature of his disease, the sovereignty of the
Turk over the Macedonians and Albanians was
purely nominal and the sufferings of the people
under his rule practically confined to the reprisals
of the soldiery upon the populace. As a neighbor
of those Balkan States who had achieved nominal
independence, the Sick Man was not very dangerous. His very incompetence was a practical guarantee of their own safety. The strengthening of
Turkey, the organization of a really efficient administration and army, whether by the Young
Turks or by the Germans, would certainly diminish the probability of securing the actual auto-

nomy which the Balkan peoples had long ardently
desired. As fast as Turkish government grew better, to that degree would disappear the grievances
which made plausible the demands of the alien
peoples for freedom from his rule. Indeed, if
many more officers were appointed of the stamp
of Hussein Kiazim Bey, the people would have
very little to complain about, and the Powers
would certainly need some strong arguments to
convince them of the expediency of permitting the
Balkan States to change the existing dispositions.
The continuance, therefore, of the present situation meant that the probability of eventual independence diminished annually and might soon
disappear.

The moment, chosen by the two coalitions as
opportune for war from their point of view, was
singularly advantageous from the point of view
of the Balkans themselves. Turkey was at war
with Italy; the real Turkish army was in Africa
and would stay there as long as the Italian fleet
controlled the sea; moreover, they were assured
by both coalitions of the nominal character of the
resistance with which the Turk would oppose
them; the war was to be a sham battle arranged
for theatrical effect. The Turks themselves were
gravely divided between the party willing to
coöperate with the Germans and the Young

Turks, anxious to strike a blow for Turkish independence before it was too late. The Balkan States had, moreover, been most kindly supplied with arms, money, and instruction in tactics and in the strategy of war by their "friends," and would therefore enter the struggle with literally every circumstance in their favor. The ease, therefore, of playing the game for themselves, of rushing upon the Turk with all possible speed, of dealing him as many deadly blows as they could as soon after the beginning of war as possible, was so apparent that there was little doubt in Sofia and Athens that the Turk would be brought to his knees before the Powers could realize that they had been betrayed. Once victorious, once possessed of the military control of Turkey, they would have their greatest chance of maintaining their independence that they ever hoped to have. If half a million men, natural soldiers, in a natural fortress, well equipped with other people's resources, could not maintain themselves against assault, independence for the Balkans was a vision which would never be attained. If they must fight to attain it, they could never have a better chance than this. But they were fully aware that the chances of their needing to fight were small. The existence of the two coalitions and the identity of their plans would convince them both that the Balkans were acting in their interests, and neither was at all likely to interfere until too late; for, when the truth of the situation should dawn upon them, it was more than likely that they would both see it simultaneously, realize that they had been hoodwinked, and be too much afraid of each other to dare to interfere. At any rate, diplomacy could be depended upon to play off the Powers one against the other. If the Balkan States could only get into their hands the strategic places, their assistance would be too vital to the completion of the schemes of both coalitions to make doubtful their ability to secure their own price. In any case, they would not be again subjected to the Turk. If they must resign themselves to the protection of one coalition or the other, they could undoubtedly secure for themselves infinitely better terms than they could otherwise have had.

Under these circumstances, the Balkan States began the war with a vigor and an energy which astounded Europe, began it, too, in the fall, contrary to the advice of both coalitions, and pushed it to a successful conclusion within a few weeks. The first result was that anticipated by the Triple Alliance, peace between Turkey and Italy, and the cession to the latter of unconditional sovereignty over Tripoli. The next results were unexpected. The war was too realistic. It was entirely undesirable for the Balkans to destroy the Turkish army which the Germans had created with so much difficulty and expense to control Constantinople and the Baghdad Railway. The Triple Entente by no means desired to hand over, even for a time, to the Balkan States Constantinople and the Straits. The first successes were probably due to the fact that the Turk was not prepared for that type of an attack, had been ordered to fall back upon Adrianople which was to be besieged. He accordingly fell back on Adrianople; the Bulgarians promptly marched round him, and fell upon the disorganized forces behind, who were as yet unprepared for operations of such magnitude. Before the Turk had time to take breath, before Berlin and Vienna recovered from the first shock, the Bulgarians were almost within sight of Constantinople, and their allies were pushing the war in the west and south to a successful conclusion with great rapidity.

It now became clear to the Balkans that the moment had come to deal with the Powers. No doubt, before the war began, the confederates had a reasonably clear idea of the terms they could expect from both coalitions, and they did not need to contemplate them longer to see that the Triple Entente was prepared to offer them vastly more satisfactory conditions. At the best, all they could hope from the Triple Alliance was the control of their local affairs; the international relations must be delivered over to the allies. The Triple Entente, on the other hand, while it would also expect to direct their international policy, found its own interests best suited by increasing the strength and independence of the Balkans themselves. Pan-Germanism, in fact, depended for its success upon their absorption by Germany and Austria, while the defeat of Pan-Germanism by the Triple Entente would depend upon the extent to which Balkan independence of Germany and Austria could be made a reality. This was certainly as virtual independence as it was probable that the possessors of such important strategic points would ever be likely to secure from the Powers. The fact that Russia's right of free passage through the Straits would in large measure satisfy her ambitions and put into her hands, without danger to the Balkan Confederation, what she chiefly valued, and what she would expect to obtain from the conquest of the whole territory, nay, what she had believed could be obtained only after the conquest of the whole territory, would give them a greater degree of assurance against aggression from her, than they could ever have from Austria. Money was another desideratum. The supply from Berlin and Vienna would obviously cease; there was no money in the Balkans and no resources which could be turned into money. To get the money, therefore, necessary to finance their independence, and, in particular, the money with which to maintain it, should they have to fight longer for it, they must sell themselves to the Triple Entente. This, they proceeded to do with dispatch, and announced in consequence that they would deal only with Turkey and would deal with her only upon the unconditional acceptance of their maximum terms. The King of Greece was to become President of the Federation, and the territory conquered from the Turk — except for Constantinople and Saloniki — was to be divided among the existing states. The Bulgarians claimed Thrace; the Greeks, Macedonia; the Servians, Albania, including the seacoast on the Adriatic. Constantinople, Saloniki, and the Straits they expected to see internationalized, the Turkish Empire relegated to Asia Minor, a freedom of passage accorded every one through the Straits. That these terms could finally be obtained, neither the Balkans nor their new allies probably believed, but that was no reason why they should not be demanded.

Undoubtedly, the war has been a great victory

for the Balkans themselves in their long crusade against the Turk. They now hope to drive the Infidel out of Europe and thus permanently to rescue their co-religionists from his clutches, both of which achievements would be supremely gratifying to them. For the present, at any rate, they are actually independent and, unless a renewal of the war should bring with it unexpected reverses, they are likely to remain so.

The chief results of the war, however, have not accrued to them but to their new allies, who have thus effectively retrieved the disaster in Tripoli. Not only will the Balkan Confederation be a stumbling-block in the path of Pan-Germanism, which is hardly likely to be moved for the present, but temporarily the alliance between the Balkans and the Triple Entente has restored the balance of power in the Mediterranean. The Greeks have driven the Italians out of most of the islands of the Ægean; Crete, which hitherto has had an anomalous existence, as an international possession, has been united to Greece and will give the Triple Entente a powerful naval station east of Malta. Above all, the loss of the islands, the certain strengthening of the English and French fleets in the Mediterranean, the improbability of Austria's taking possession of Saloniki for some time to come, have greatly reduced the chances of the use of Tripoli as a military and naval base. Certainly, until the Austrians and Italians are prepared to contest the supremacy of the Mediterranean, the Italians will have only such relations with Tripoli as the English permit. The latter are not likely to bring the question of Italy's right to Tripoli to a test of force, but they will no doubt feel themselves justified in preventing her from attempting anything beyond the commercial development of the country.

The interposition of the Balkan Confederation between Austria and Turkey has for the time being deprived the Germans of communication with Turkey and has jeopardized their control of the Baghdad Railway. The Turk, excluded from Europe, robbed of his most valuable possession, the Straits, would not be as available material from the German point of view as he was. The new Turkish army, if we suppose that it was safe and sound in Tripoli and was not shot to pieces in the war, would no longer be as valuable as when it could hope to guard the trade route from Constantinople well through the mountains, protecting Constantinople itself and the Baghdad Railway. The importance of protecting the railway may still be great, but the commercial importance of its protection can amount to very

little so long as the trade route has been cut apart
in the middle. Not improbably commercial treaties can be signed with the Balkans, but if the latter
are able to maintain their present position either by
extorting favorable terms from the reluctant Turk
or by a renewal of the war, such treaties will be
subject to rupture at a moment's notice. The
expediency may well be questioned of spending
money in the development of Asia Minor by a
power which can obtain access to the district only
by the sufferance of states hostile to her ambitions.

These significant changes of strategic position
led both the Triple Alliance and the Turks to
offer terms of peace so remote from the demands
of the Balkan States as to evoke from the latters'
representatives at the negotiations opened at
London in December, 1912, the excited cry that
the Turkish proposals did not even provide a basis
for compromise and practically ignored the vic-
tories of the allies. The Turkish proposals were in
very truth nothing more nor less than the salient
features of the plan of the Triple Alliance for the
reorganization of south-eastern Europe which
would have been executed had the Balkan States
remained faithful and conquered Turkey as at
first arranged. Such terms would, indeed, rob
the victors of the spoils; would create new autonomous states out of the territory just conquered,

and, injury of injuries, would actually leave the
new states under Turkish suzerainty. Such offers
were rightly interpreted as defiance, as unwilling-
ness to accept the most obvious facts of the military situation.

In addition, the Albanians were persuaded by
Austrian promises of support to declare themselves independent, and Servia saw her access to
the Adriatic, the dearest of her ambitions, her
chief reason for joining in the war at all, snatched
from her. At Vienna, however, it was felt that immediate war would be preferable to the surrender
of Albania and the shores of the lower Adriatic
to any such confederation supported by the
Triple Entente. Vigorous diplomatic representations were followed by the mobilization of Austrian
army corps and of the Danube fleet. In the face
of this determination, both the Triple Entente
and Servia judged it best to agree to the independence of Albania, and for Servia to obtain
access to the Adriatic by means of a railway
whose neutrality would be secured by international agreement.

But upon the destruction of the Turkish power
in Europe, the Balkans insisted, and were secretly
supported by the Triple Entente, which hoped
thus to destroy one more link of the chain of
Pan-Germanism. The Balkan States, therefore,

demanded the surrender of most of Thrace and in particular of the great fortress of Adrianople, whose possession would expose Constantinople to assault at any time and leave the Turk a bare foothold on the Bosphorus, of which he could at any time be deprived. Besides, unless Thrace were obtained, there would be no territory to be won by the Bulgarians, who had done most of the fighting, for the Greeks obstinately declined to share Macedonia with them. If Adrianople could not be secured without further fighting, it was clearly to the interests of the Balkans and their allies to renew the war.

On the other hand, for the Turks to yield Adrianople, without further fighting, would mean for Germany and Austria the unresisting acquiescence in the virtual failure of Pan-Germanism by permitting the interposition of a permanent barrier between them and Asia Minor, which would compel them to relinquish Turkey, Constantinople, the control of the Straits, the Baghdad Railway, and the commercial route to the East at one fell swoop. To have lost the Balkans was disastrous; to lose Constantinople as well would be the death-knell of Pan-Germanism. They are therefore in favor of allowing the Turk to fight again.

Nor is the Turk unwilling. The Young Turks are well aware that the new Turkish army, trained by Von der Göltz, has not yet been in battle, and, until it has been defeated, they decline to surrender as much as they might lose if their whole army had been annihilated in a long, hard-fought war. Have they not already beaten the Greeks? Have they not checked the Italian advance in Tripoli? Above all, these fresh troops, well equipped, will meet an army decimated by its recklessness in earlier battles, with resources seriously impaired by a long campaign and a long armistice, and with its lines of communication blocked by snow and ice.

At the moment of writing, therefore, January 19, 1913, the renewal of the war seems more likely to further the interests of all concerned than the adoption of any terms yet proposed. The actual inability of Germany or Austria to finance the war for Turkey or to supply her with arms and ammunition may force the latter to yield, and will in all probability prevent prolonged resistance. Certainly, Austria's inability to float a relatively small loan in Europe and the sale of the bonds in New York at an interest rate of seven per cent, demonstrates conclusively the financial stringency in Austria, Germany, and Italy. It really seems as if the control of the financial world by the Triple Entente had again defeated the Triple Alliance, for the latter is recommending the Turks to cede Adrianople.

For all these reasons, it is highly unlikely that the Triple Alliance will attempt in the immediate future any movement to alter the situation by direct intervention in the Balkans. The Confederation is too strong in men, too strongly entrenched to make military operations anything but hazardous, even had they no aid to expect from Russia. The whole of Europe is too well prepared to risk a general war at present. Modern warfare is of such character that the element of surprise in an attack is almost certain to conclude the war in the aggressor's favor, while an attack upon a nation fully prepared to receive it becomes under modern conditions inevitably hazardous. Besides, it is by no means clear at the present moment that the Triple Alliance is strong enough in armies and navies to boast an even chance of victory in a contest with the Triple Entente. They will, therefore, if again defeated after the renewal of war, be likely to conceal their chagrin as best they can, accept such losses of strategic position as diplomacy cannot avoid, and hope that some opportunity will appear in the near future of discovering a price, which they can afford to pay the Balkans, and which the latter will consider a sufficient inducement, to make it worth their while to change sides. Indeed, the stronger the Balkan Confederation, the more independent, the greater factor it will become in European affairs, the more difficult it will become for either coalition to act without its support, the more active will become their bidding for its favor, the more difficult it will become for either of them to interfere in that district by force.

The vital difficulty in perpetuating the new Balkan Confederacy is that the governmental lines as they are now drawn do not coincide with the most important racial and religious lines. Bosnia, Herzegovina, and the Illyrian coast, which are now part of Austria, belong racially, religiously, and geographically with Servia. Much of Hungary similarly ought to be connected with Rumania, while Albania contains so many races and creeds that it does not really belong anywhere. It must not be forgotten, too, in considering the ease of separating the Balkan Confederation into its component parts by the diplomacy of either coalition, that the Balkans have long been the scene of a blood feud between the Mohammedans and Christians, many of whom will inevitably remain in their present positions, and that in the Balkans continues at present the active struggle for supremacy between the Greek and Latin branches of the Christian Church. The hatred of the Greeks in Servia and in Bulgaria was until recently intense, and, however

228

these varied states may have compromised at present their various jarring ambitions, or have buried for the time being their traditional hatreds, once the Turk is thoroughly disposed of, and they settle down to the difficult task of living with each other, they are more than likely to fall at loggerheads over the inevitable administrative and governmental questions involved in the institution of a permanent settlement. If the treaty of peace hands over Macedonia to Greece, it is hardly likely that the diplomats will succeed in demarcating the limits of that hitherto elastic province in a fashion which will satisfy more than a fraction of those interested. There are so many quasilogical and reasonable methods of separating it from Servia, Bulgaria, and Greece, that none of them are likely to meet the wishes of all concerned. The present Balkan unity is based upon their hatred of the Turk and their fears of European interference. When once their autonomy is definitely assured, both of these bonds will disappear, and the lack of geographical, religious, racial, administrative, economic unity of any kind, sort, or description will inevitably begin to manifest itself in ways which cannot be foreseen, and which cannot fail to test to the utmost the sanity and ability of the native statesman.

CHAPTER XV

THE JUSTIFIABILITY OF PAN-GERMANISM

ANY consideration, however slight or casual, of the justifiability of so far-reaching a plan as Pan-Germanism must necessarily begin with the validity of the standard to be employed in judging it. Even a comparatively slight acquaintance with history will make sufficiently evident the existence in the world of politics and business of a different standard from that criterion of absolute truth which we ordinarily apply to the conduct of individuals. We find, in fact, that same double standard in existence in international politics which is so perplexing to the majority of men in connection with every-day business, where the usual conception of ethics declares it right for one man to best the other by any means he can, short of actual violence and the actual breach of the letter of the law. The majority of men, whatever professions they are willing to make verbally, do not practice the Golden Rule or the Sermon on the Mount. If we apply to the situation in international politics the ethical and moral tenets, frankly professed by the community, and,

as frankly, disregarded in every-day life, we shall
necessarily conclude that Pan-Germanism is not
and never can be justifiable. If we proceed, too,
in attempting to evaluate the moral and ethical
aspects of Pan-Germanism, from the position in
regard to war assumed by the numerous societies
advocating international peace or arbitration,
we shall also be in danger of assuming the truth
of our conclusion as our premise. The advocates
of peace declare that war is cruel, brutal, economically wasteful, and, from every point of view,
opposed to the true interests of the community
as a whole and of the individuals who compose it.
They declaim against it as foolish; who would
really be so lacking in reason as to suppose that
the truth and justice of great questions could
be established by fighting? Such men must still
be dwelling mentally in the darkness of remote
antiquity. They insist that war is void of good
result; who can be so lost to all sense of proportion and value as to suppose that destruction can
be constructive? To argue from any such premises
as these will be necessarily to establish that any
such scheme of aggression as that proposed by
Germany is not only lacking in morality but in
sanity.

The candid student, however, who is not anxious to support a propaganda, and who seeks

rather to explain and expound the real reasons
which have led men into such paths as they are
now following than to cavil and blame, will recognize in Pan-Germanism the expression of a national determination to preserve and strengthen
the corporate life of a great people. Its basis is
greed from one point of view, ambition from another, but its effective cause in both cases is the
expression of nationality. Germany, in fact, has
attained a national consciousness, a national in-
dividuality, and seeks to insure the continued existence of this corporate individual for all time.
Pan-Germanism is merely self-preservation. This
new individual, who entered the world through
the travail of the nineteenth century, is conscious
of his sturdy strength and of his growing needs, is
ambitious to improve his own condition and to
leave to those who come after him a solid guarantee of immunity from the suffering and priva-
tion that he has endured. Above all, he is filled
with an uncontrollable determination to establish
his economic well-being. With growth have come
new economic wants, which have in turn revealed
the existence of hitherto unexpected desires,
clamoring for satisfaction and to be satisfied only
by the increased wealth which depends in its own
turn upon the possibility of national expansion.
Unquestionably, the creation of this corporate

individual is the result of the working of natural forces, present in the life of every European community, and to whose operation every nation in Europe owes that degree of prosperity and corporate consciousness which it possesses. To a greater or less degree, all are actuated by the motives which influence Germany. It is by no means clear that, if their circumstances were identical with hers, they would fail to employ all the methods of which she is ready to avail herself. Whether or not we are willing to admit that there are moral and ethical principles of permanent value, absolutely binding upon all individuals and communities from century to century, we cannot deny that the record of the past amply proves that no nation has yet refrained, because of moral scruples, from advancing its economic or national welfare by any means it could. If Germany is wrong, others too have been wrong; indeed, if her conduct is unjustifiable, no country in the world can establish its moral and ethical right to existence. At the same time that we recognize the recrudescence of certain factors familiar to all situations, we must not be blind to the vastly more important fact that the present situation is literally without precedent in the history of the world.

The present international situation is the result

of the economic progress of the last half-century. The improvements in agriculture, in manufacturing, in transportation, have for the first time since man began to write the record of his deeds made the world capable of more than keeping itself in existence. The increased production of food and clothes, entirely beyond any immediate needs of the existing community, has stimulated to an unprecedented degree the growth of population, while the progress of industry and agriculture has as constantly out-distanced the increasing population. The satiation of the old economic wants of the individual, for food, clothes, and shelter, produced inevitably new standards of well-being which declared subsistence to be something more than the ability to keep alive, and which insisted upon a certain excellence of quality in the food and clothes, a certain amount of leisure for amusement and self-culture, a certain degree of education. The luxuries of preceding centuries became necessities. More economic wants appeared. Men whose ancestors had been well content with one good meal a day and a thatched cottage of one room are demanding a house with glass windows and three liberal meals a day, including fresh meat, beverages, sugar, and butter. While few will claim that the new standard is excessive, no candid student can deny the astonishing increase in the number of economic wants never before felt by so large a proportion of the community.

To continue to feed and clothe the growing multitudes, to meet the demands imposed upon industry and agriculture by the new standards of living, an approximate utilization of all the resources of the community became necessary. In the past the vastness of the resources of the globe had never been suspected; agriculture had merely scratched the ground; mines had been worked only where large deposits of comparatively free metal lay near the surface; manufacturing, so far as the majority of the community was concerned, had been confined to the production of rough cloth and the absolute essentials of existence. The substitution of machines for the thousands of hands needed in the past for the performance of the same task, the utilization of the resources of the community in anything like an adequate way for the first time, enabled a part of the community to supply the whole with the necessities of life, even according to the new standard of living, and, therefore, enabled the remainder to devote their time to less essential tasks. Many of them turned their attention to meeting the new economic wants, others occupied their time by still further developing the economic possibilities of the community. And for the first time in history, it became possible for vast numbers of men to turn their attention solely to the furtherance of the community's ambitions. Hitherto no standing army of considerable size could be maintained in Europe, for the simple reason that so large a number of hands could not be spared from the fields from which the community derived its maintenance. Nor were the transportation facilities adequate to provide these men with a steady supply of food and clothes during the necessary period of training. A standing army of hundreds of thousands of men, who devote their whole time to learning the art of war, and who are maintained by the state during their apprenticeship, is a phenomenon which nothing short of the economic progress of the last half-century could have made possible. For the first time enough men can be spared from the task of keeping the community alive to devote themselves to the prosecution of a war founded only in aggression. Pan-Germanism has been made possible by the economic growth of the nineteenth century.

Paradoxical as it may sound, the internal peace of Europe since 1815, except for sporadic outbreaks here and there, has intensified in degree this new phase of national activity. Hitherto, the resources of every country, in men and in food, were periodically reduced by famine and pesti-

lence, and, above all, by the destructive nature
of war as it was necessarily prosecuted before the
modern railway made it possible to supply an
army from a distance. The same lack of transportation, which forced the soldiers to forage on
the country, also forced each district of the country to depend, almost entirely, in time of peace
upon its own efforts for its own subsistence.
Floods, drought, blight, various diseases of cattle,
produced famine and the inevitable reduction of
the population, often in the same little community
not less frequently than twice or thrice within a
generation. Under these circumstances the ability of a country to go to war, to put men into its
army, to divert them from the fields, even during
the continuance of the war, depended upon its
comparative freedom from these artificial methods of losing its strength. The comparative peace
of the last century and the progress of medical
science, as well as the advance in agriculture and
industry, have enormously strengthened the nations of the world by giving them a surplus of
men and materials, which they can now devote to
the prosecution of a war of aggression without
endangering the lives of those already in existence.
Moreover, this same peace, which has greatly
contributed to the unprecedented increase of
population and of wealth, and which has per-

mitted the devotion of so much time and labor
to the satisfaction of economic wants which past
centuries would have considered superficial, is
in no small measure responsible for that very
economic pressure of population, that need of an
outlet for the swelling surplus of manufactures
which is driving Germany, Austria, and Italy into
this great scheme of aggression. Their present
resources, their ability to support themselves by
the labors of a fraction of the community, which
permit them to undertake such aggression, are
the very factors which make expansion inevitable. The interaction and the interrelation of
these varied economic factors have produced not
only the impulse but the means of satisfying it.

The unprecedented growth of population in all
countries of Europe, which has compelled them
to utilize their resources as never before, has not
expanded their boundaries. Germany has substantially no more arable land available than in
1815. The erasure of traditional boundaries, the
disappearance of administrative and legal factors
familiar to the past, does not alter the vital fact
that the Germanic race still occupies to all intents
and purposes the same territory it held in the
year 1500. It is, in fact, in the feeling of limitation,
engendered by the extent to which the present
natural resources of Europe have been drawn

the newspaper, have created the modern nation of whose ambition and strength these schemes of aggression are merely the expression. The peoples of the past centuries lived in isolation, never conscious of what was happening at that same moment elsewhere, rarely able to act in concert for lack of that knowledge. The great movements of history have been limited to small areas, to a few men, because of the impossibility of securing the coöperation of a greater number. Time used to be absolutely a prerequisite for any movement whatever, and there was no means of promptly communicating with every one, or of discovering, soon enough to be of practical value, the sentiments of different sections of the community. The intensification of national feeling, — one might almost say the creation for the first time of a truly national feeling, — the possibility for the first time of so large an aggregation of individuals having anything resembling unity of thought and feeling, has created the present crisis and is its most salient feature. Each nation, thus more acutely conscious of itself and more keenly conscious of the conditions which support it, has become more acutely conscious of others and has felt more keenly the differences in development, in economic status, in intellectual progress, in artistic achievement, which distinguish it from its neighbors. The extent and possible variety of interests are dawning upon the national consciousness for perhaps the first time with anything like adequacy, and with it, also for the first time, there is dawning in the minds of all nations some faint adumbration of the glorious national future before a people capable, really and literally, of acting, thinking, and feeling as one. Indeed, the vision has roused men from the contemplation of their own petty doings and lifted them into a sphere broader and more impersonal. For a great people, who had become conscious of such a unity of feeling, of such a dependence upon each other, and of the possibilities of united action, nothing is more normal than to attempt, by the exercise of forethought, to increase the strength, capacity, and influence of this corporate body, to knit it more firmly together, to place it upon a still more solid basis of economic prosperity. Nor is it strange that the first ecstasy of national consciousness should have brought with it fears for its own continuance and a passionate desire to insure that continuance for all time. Indeed, it is probably no exaggeration to claim that the present aggressive schemes of most European nations are soberly intended to preserve what exists rather than to increase it, even though by preservation they mean no mere continued existence, but the absolute assurance of the existence of a prosperous, enlightened nation for the rest of time.

One trouble which most students seem to experience in attempting to judge the present crisis arises from the tendency to assume that the greatest good is to be insured by the preservation of the conditions now in existence. One might almost say that the advocates of peace tend to regard the present *status quo* as the end and object of the process of evolution. They seem, in fact, to oppose, or at least to deprecate, the persistent attempts of mankind to accelerate the pace of civilization, and to desire to limit the tools which men are to use in the future to economic weapons. Probably this phase of contemporary thought is a part of the natural reaction from the logical consequences of the doctrine of evolution as expounded by Spencer. To their thinking, the relegation of the influence exerted by moral and ethical forces to the second rank proceeds from a failure to appreciate their real force, and they are consequently drawn into an aggressive assertion of the superiority of mind over matter, of the spiritual over the physical, among those varied forces to whose operation the development of society has been due. One can hardly study the modern situation, however, without becoming keenly aware that the difference between war and peace, as the words are ordinarily used, is rather one of degree and of outward form than of purpose. The nations of the world have unquestionably been busy for the last half-century with the determined attempt to surpass each other, to get possession of things which they did not have already, by methods which rest certainly upon the same ethical foundation that war does, and whose results upon the individual, and even upon nations, are not necessarily different in kind from those of actual warfare. To be sure, the financial operations known as peaceful penetration are not exactly what we have been accustomed to consider methods of violent conquest; but by such means large numbers of the inhabitants of the smaller countries have just as certainly lost their land and the products of their labor as if an army had destroyed them. There is perhaps a nice discrimination to be drawn by some logician between taking a man's property away from him or stealing a nation's independence by means of an army and by means of high finance; but if the individual or the nation suffers the same loss from both processes, and if the intent is essentially the same, it is difficult to see where the ethical grounds supporting them differ. If it would be wicked for Germany to enter Belgium with an army and take possession of the country, seizing the revenues and compelling the Belgians to accept from them loans of money at such terms that the Belgians would practically lose possession of their own government for half a century to come, why is it more moral for France to obtain the same results in Morocco, or for the United States in a similar manner to secure possession of Mexico and Central America, so that the inhabitants have scarcely anything left to call their own but their very lives? Indeed, there are more ways of conquest than fighting, and more methods of robbery than the Middle Ages were familiar with.

It must be admitted in all candor that the impulses behind Pan-Germanism exist at present in all nations, and that no nation is likely at present to forego the possibility of future development because of even the most plausible ethical or logical pleas. The three nations, who have entered into the promotion of Pan-Germanism, are not different from the others in morals or in aims. Their geographical position, their peculiar economic fabric, the traditions of their past, all force upon them the aggressive part and make immediate action desirable. England, France, Russia, and the United States already possess the choice places in the world; their position is already everything they could reasonably hope to have it; and they scarcely deserve to be praised for unselfishness when they insist upon preserving a situation which is so very much to their advantage. Obviously, their national existence and ambition will be best furthered by the continuance of the *status quo*, because they will thus be able to keep what they already hold. Nor is it proved that they have obtained it by the observance of the ethical precepts which they would now be glad to apply to Germany; they secured their empires, in fact, by precisely those methods which Germany wishes to use against them. It is as selfish for them to insist upon peace as it is for the Germans to demand war. In reality, the difference of opinion as to the proper procedure for settling the difficulty is not based upon ethical concepts at all. It merely means that the Triple Entente prefers to employ in the struggle only the economic and financial weapons in whose use they are already adepts and of which they already possess so many more than their rivals as to make the outcome of the struggle, if fought on this basis, practically positive to be in their favor. The Triple Entente, in fact, like the good Doctor Franchard, have derived their philosophy from their desires, and have painted a picture of the millennium of peace whose lineaments are necessarily those of their present condition. Germany, Austria, and Italy, conscious of their disadvantage on the economic plane, are anxious to employ in the coming duel a different type of weapon, in whose use they believe themselves more expert than are their enemies.

One might almost compare the two coalitions with a trained swordsman and a countryman who have somehow gotten into a quarrel. The swordsman wishes to settle the point of honor by a duel with rapiers under limitations which require the combatants to employ only one arm and to use only the point, to attack only after due warning, and not to press the adversary to the utmost. These conditions condemn the countryman to defeat. He wishes to fight with his fists, to hit wherever he can and as often as possible, to give no quarter, and to continue the fight until one or the other is exhausted. The swordsman, gazing upon the brawny figure of his opponent, is afraid that, in a struggle of that nature, he might not be successful, and hesitates to stake his all upon a rough-and-tumble battle. He insists upon fighting like a gentleman, and talks about honor, and ethics, and the obligations of civilization. The countryman sees plainly enough that all this is intended to rob him of an advantage, and he, therefore, declines to be bound by a variety of ethics or a code of morals which necessarily condemn him to defeat.

So of the two coalitions; the Triple Entente,

with so much to lose, is most anxious to avoid an appeal to fisticuffs, and wishes, if possible, to limit the weapons, and thus the extent of defeat. The Triple Alliance, with little likelihood of succeeding, but with nearly everything to gain if it should succeed, is a great deal more willing to appeal to the ultimate arbitrament of war. As a matter of fact, they regard war as their last chance. They have fought the Triple Entente with economic weapons for a good deal more than a generation and are not yet within measurable distance of victory. If, then, we regard the truth as a concept which becomes gradually visible as we study the record of the past, if moral concepts are not those which men proclaim but those by which they live, we shall be forced to admit that the Triple Alliance is not morally worse than the Triple Entente. Certainly, the validity of such standards in such circumstances as their adversaries wish to apply has never yet been admitted by any nation within the ken of history. The Germans refuse, therefore, to accept an adverse judgment based upon standards which cannot claim general acceptance by the Congress of Nations.

CHAPTER XVI

THE PROBABILITY OF THE SUCCESS OF PAN-GERMANISM

I. *Internal Weaknesses*

THE most interesting phase of the present international situation to the vast majority of people comprises those considerations which serve in one way or another as indications of the probable success or failure of the schemes at present advocated by the two great coalitions. As has already been said, the success of Pan-Germanism will depend upon the truth or falsity of the German notions of the situation in Europe, upon the verity of their ideas regarding the proportional strength of the various nations and the adequacy of the methods they have devised for taking advantage of what they believe to be a superior position. In the chapters devoted to an exposition of the German view of the present situation, the factors in their favor were described as fully as is possible in so brief an account as this. Nor is there a great deal of doubt in the impartial student's mind regarding the substantial truth of the propositions there laid down. The strong points of the German case are naturally those whose truth is not likely to be contested, and, in order to put the case forcibly enough to carry conviction to the ordinary Anglo-Saxon, it seemed better to group strong facts and to postpone for the time a discussion of weaknesses. While it is probable that the Germans exaggerate the degree of their own strength and the extent of England's weakness, while it is probable that they rely too much upon the assumed difference in efficiency between their administration and that of France and Russia, it cannot be gainsaid by a candid observer that on the whole the Germans' notion of the proportional supremacy of the various nations and in particular their ideas of English history are substantially correct. Indeed, no one has stated these propositions with greater force than Professor Seeley, whose "Expansion of England" appeared at just the time when Pan-Germanism was in the making. England is no longer defended by the Channel as she once was; she certainly never took possession of her dependencies by actual conquest, nor does she retain possession by means of physical force; the self-governing colonies are manifestly without geographical contiguity, and have been independent in all but name for the better part of a century. The weakness of England's long chain of strate-

gic points has always been apparent to its pos-
sessor; but, so long as it served the purpose for
which it was constructed, there was no reason for
abandoning it simply because certain conditions
might render it vulnerable.

The Germans also correctly appreciate the fact
that an English victory in a naval war will simply
maintain the position which she already holds; a
defeat they also see will be fatal to her; in a naval
war she has comparatively little to gain, while
they may win everything. To their thinking this
balances the scales very much in their favor. To
reach them, the English must have recourse to land
warfare for which they are not really fitted, and
not well placed, since the true base of the English
position against Germany, so far as the offensive
is concerned, is the frontier between Germany and
Belgium and Holland. From a military point of
view, the seizure of these two countries by Germany at the moment of the outbreak of war would
move the Germans into what is properly speaking
English territory and demolish important obsta-
cles in the way of an attack upon England's most
vital spot. There seems to be some truth in the
German view that Russia and France are not as
capable as she of utilizing their full resources
with promptitude. It is extremely probable that
most nations in the world would be very glad to

assist in looting the British Empire. Certainly the German scheme for taking possession of her own lands and factories, which have been developed with borrowed money, has been executed before in similar cases with undoubtedly disastrous results to the borrowers. It has never been consciously attempted on so huge a scale. The potency of the economic weapons which she believes can be brought to bear upon England and France is undoubted, but there seem to be a good many difficulties in the way of putting such forces into effective operation. In short, on its face the German scheme is not only feasible but conclusive. Theoretically there are no flaws.

In attempting to render judgment upon so stupendous an enterprise, we must not forget that, as students, we are really not in a position to render more than an approximate judgment, because we cannot be at all certain that we know all the essential details, or that we know the truth about factors of such evident importance as the efficiency of armies and navies, the real economic strength of the countries, the actual situation of forts and batteries. We cannot in the nature of things have more than an approximate idea of the scheme itself or of the conditions on which it is based, and we therefore must be content with a very approximate judgment. The really satisfactory evidence in favor of the feasibility of Pan-Germanism is to be found in the obvious fact that the statesmen and diplomats of Europe, who know more about the situation than historians ever will, believe that its success is probable. There can be no doubt that the leaders in Germany, Austria, and Italy have believed in the certainty of its eventual success for more than a generation. The evident fears and public avowals of imminent danger threatening the members of the Triple Entente is conclusive proof that they too consider it feasible.[1] Another earnest of its possibility is to be found in the degree of completion already attained. In the fall of the year 1912 it looked for a week or two as if the Pan-German confederation had actually come into existence. It was certainly within measurable distance of completion. Than this no better evidence is available.

When, however, we write of the success of Pan-Germanism, we mean something more complex than at first may appear. Pan-Germanism involves the creation of the confederation of states which it intends to make the controlling factor in international politics; it involves, in the next place, the ability of this confederation to get con-

[1] See the speech of Premier Borden of Canada advocating a new naval policy and the Official Memorandum of the English Admiralty on England's present and future naval position, both of which are printed in the Appendix.

trol of the world or at least to defeat England;
it further assumes the feasibility of maintaining
control and of preserving its own existence against
internal as well as external foes. The Germans
are apparently ready to assume the ease of creating the confederation and devote their attention
chiefly to the possibility of securing control of the
world, should they succeed in developing their own
offensive strength in the manner proposed. All
the conditions advanced about England's weakness and the inefficiency of France and Russia
bear upon the second of these three propositions,
and have little or nothing to do with the first and
third. This is the real weakness of Pan-Germanism. If we are not led astray by the fact that
we probably are not permitted to know as much
about the German plans for accomplishing the
first and third of these objects as they are ready to
tell us about the premises upon which the second
depends, it is upon this rock that the scheme will
probably be wrecked. It cannot be too often said,
however, that the statements in regard to the
weakness of her enemies have been promulgated
with a frequency and decisiveness, which lends
color to the assumption that they were made with
official sanction for the sake of the moral effect
that they would have in Germany and particularly
in other parts of the world. Undoubtedly, the

difficulties of creating the confederation at all are better known in Berlin and Vienna than we can possibly envisage them; the certain difficulties of maintaining control of the world, once it is obtained, cannot fail to have caused the statesmen of the Triple Alliance many anxious hours. Naturally, they are less ready to call attention to such aspects of the plan than they are to the more obvious factors where the verdict of history and the testimony of their own enemies prove them to be right.

Pan-Germanism, in fact, is weakest at its centre. Its success is least probable at home. Without the coöperation of Austria and Italy, the scheme is impossible, and scarcely two generations ago the enmity between the three allies led them into war with each other. Austria and Prussia have hated each other throughout history with a vigor scarcely surpassed by the hatred which Prussia bears France. Indeed, when Bismarck was first in Vienna he doubted his own safety. The Italians have by no means lost their distrust of Austria, and it is really probable that the first successes gained by the alliance may result in such accessions of strength to one or more of the allies as to rouse the jealousies and apprehensions of the others. The notion of putting into Austria's hands the whole eastern coast of the Adriatic

is extremely distasteful to Italy, and certainly
would place Austria in a strong position, from
which the conquest of the Po Valley would be
undoubtedly feasible. There are vital differences,
therefore, between the three contracting countries.

Moreover, Prussia and Austria are thoroughly
well hated in southern Germany. The comic
papers of Munich are fond of printing scandal-
ous cartoons and squibs about the emperors; it is
popularly supposed that neither emperor would
dare venture into southern Germany without a
large bodyguard. It must not be forgotten that
the German Constitution gives the southern
states important military privileges, which could
not fail to be of consequence in time of war.
Furthermore, southern Germany controls important approaches to Alsace, the passes through
Switzerland, and the whole upper half of the
Rhine and Danube valleys. In Alsace and Lorraine public feeling against Prussia is exceedingly
strong; at a recent public meeting, an official
openly turned the Emperor's statue with its face to
the wall amid pretty general and open expressions
of approval. The recent erection and dedication
of a German statue at Metz, commemorating
battles of the Franco-Prussian War, was, to say
the least, unfortunate in its effect upon public
opinion. The incidents given by Stevenson in

his "Inland Voyage" are enlightening as to the sentiments of the people who occupy the strategic point of greatest importance to Prussia: "In the morning a hawker and his wife went down the street at a foot pace singing to a very slow, lamentable music, 'O France, mes amours.' It brought everybody to the door, and when our landlady called in the man to buy the words, he had not a copy of them left. . . . I have watched a forester from Alsace, while some one was singing 'Les malheurs de la France,' at a baptismal party. . . . He arose from the table and took his son aside, close by where I was standing. 'Listen, listen,' he said, bearing on the boy's shoulder, 'and remember this, my son.' A little after he went out into the garden suddenly, and I could hear him sobbing in the darkness. In what other country will you find a patriotic ditty bring all the world into the street?"

The efficiency of Austria in the coming generation, the possibility of maintaining its position in Europe and of contributing strength to the Triple Alliance, depend upon the ability of the present rulers to maintain the present relations between Austria and Hungary and between the various sections of the Austrian Empire. There is perhaps no part of Europe where racial feeling is so intense or where so many races are juxtaposited.

Their quarrels have filled the history of Europe with discord; the number of irreconcilables, who wish to overthrow the present government and to substitute for it anything else whatever, is extremely large, and seems to be increasing rather than decreasing. Hungary hates Austria; Bohemia wishes to be independent; the Slavs and Croatians in the southwest have agitated independence for generations; the Ruthenes and the Poles in the northeast are equally determined to submit to Austrian rule no longer than they must. In Hungary, the struggle of the Magyars to retain their racial supremacy is of the keenest, and constantly results in violent outbreaks and riots.[1] So slight a thing as the posting of a sign in one language or another over a railway station has been known to result in a riot of nearly the proportions of a civil war. Recently when the Italian students at the University of Vienna undertook to celebrate one of their national holidays, the German and the Austrian students attempted to put a stop to it by force. The police interfered; were met by armed resistance from the students; and it was for some days doubtful whether peace could be preserved by the military in one of the greatest capitals in Europe. Surely a pitched

[1] "Even in quiet times the Magyar will get the gypsies to play him the song, 'The German is a blackguard.'" Bismarck, *Reflections and Reminiscences*, II, 257.

battle between Italians, Austrians, and Germans arising out of racial and national feeling, fought in the streets of Vienna, is a sinister omen in the path of Pan-Germanism. It has been widely proclaimed by both the initiated and the uninitiated that Austria-Hungary has been held together for more than a decade simply because the various warring elements have been waiting for the death of the present Emperor to give the signal for revolt. Surely, when the student considers the relative international weakness or national strength of the countries of Europe, it will be difficult for him to value Austria-Hungary at anything above the minimum figure.

The great district known as the Balkans is an absolutely essential factor of the Pan-German confederation, yet there is no part of all Europe which lacks more conspicuously geographical, political, and racial unity. The Balkans include all the land stretching from the water parting of the Tyrolese and Transylvanian Alps to the Mediterranean and the Ægean, — the rich plains of the Lower Danube, the tablelands and mountain valleys of Macedonia and Servia, the wild crags of Montenegro and Albania. The people range from stolid peasantry in the valleys to wild, scarcely civilized hillmen in the west and the intelligent cultivated citizens of Sofia and Athens.

PAN-GERMANISM

The racial admixture is extraordinary in its variety and distribution. There are many districts where no single race can boast predominance. For centuries the Balkans have been the seat of the most intense religious hatred in Europe and are the only states where active warfare still continues between the Christian and the Infidel and between the Latin and Greek Churches. There are not a few districts where, as in Albania, the Mohammedan, the Greek Christian, and the Catholic live so near one another as to result in constant reprisals which keep the community in a condition of alarm and anxiety. The problem of creating amid such conditions, out of such varied races, whose religious and racial hatreds and antipathies are so intense, a strong series of states which will act in concert with the Triple Alliance in the execution of so complicated a scheme as Pan-Germanism, would seem to the observer to border upon impossibility. The Balkans hate each other so cordially, the states which have attained politicial existence contain within their own borders so many elements of discord, that it might almost be claimed that the only elements of unity are the vigorous hatred that they all bear the Turk and the intense suspicion with which they all regard Austria and Russia.

Yet, through these defiles run the great roads connecting Europe and Asia, along which the trade of centuries has passed, and which must still continue to be the channels of overland communication with the East. The Balkans hold the eastern side of the Adriatic, the western shore of the Black Sea, the whole lower course of the Danube, and two sides of the Ægean. If the Triple Alliance ever expects to obtain a position of importance in the Mediterranean, it must possess them. Yet the dream of the peoples in those valleys and plains is for autonomy, freedom from European interference, the exclusion of the religious, strategic, political interests of other nations, the recognition of their right to live for themselves. To use these peoples in the formation of the Pan-German confederation means and will continue to mean their armament by Austria and Germany, the financing of their preparations for war, — in fact, the placing in their hands of weapons which will be exactly as useful against the Triple Alliance as against the Triple Entente. The creation in the Balkans of a confederation of states of the type desired by Austria and Germany is perhaps possible and may be, indeed, feasible; but the preservation of the control of the Triple Alliance over those states, once created, the ability of the statesmen in Berlin and Vienna to rouse in those

PAN–GERMANISM

peoples any enthusiasm for Pan-Germanism, seems highly improbable. At the present moment of writing, it looks as if a confederation hostile to the Triple Alliance had been formed, which is probably strong enough to maintain itself for some decades. The conquest of the Balkans by Austria would be no easy matter. The land itself is a natural fortress, improved by Austrian and German engineers in all those varied ways which modern warfare has made possible, and the batteries have been erected on the borders between Austria and the Balkans as well as on the south. This was the price which the Balkan States demanded in exchange for the coöperation which they promised: they must be provided with weapons which would assure their independence even of Austria. The people are natural soldiers, carefully drilled, well equipped, flushed at present with victory, and fired with the determination to maintain their independence against all comers. Nothing could possibly be more detrimental to the interests of Pan-Germanism, and it seems to be a difficulty which nothing short of years can remove. The position of the Balkans, should they maintain it, would be definitive in bringing about the failure of Pan-Germanism.

The last link in the German chain, the first one they attempted to create, is Turkey. The natural ineptitude of the Turkish Government has become a byword of statesmen; the Turks are alien in race and religion to the majority of the subject peoples; their hatred for the Christians is still intense; and the difficulty, therefore, of conducting operations through their hands is great. That, however, might be overcome had the Turk continued supine. The real difficulty which at present stands in the way of the establishment of German control in Turkey is the rise among the Turks of a national party whose chief aim is the exclusion of the foreigner and the government of Turkey solely in the interest of the Turk. Under this banner have been enlisted the majority, at any rate, of the Turks intelligent enough to be entrusted with the administration of their own country. The mere fact that they are an insignificant minority of the population, that the rest of the Turks have no effective desire for self-government and are certainly not capable of it, does not in the least change the significant fact that the only Turks who might govern their country, as the Germans wish it done, decline the task. Indeed, the Young Turks assisted the German plans and created the present government, with the idea that Germany would allow them to rule the rest of their countrymen. Their disappointment was exceedingly bitter when they learned that the real direction of policy and the control of finance was to rest with the German officials in Constantinople. The probable disappearance of European Turkey as a result of the Balkan War will certainly increase the difficulty the Germans have already experienced.

The problem of Pan-Germanism in Turkey is not as serious as it is in Austria, in Hungary, and in the Balkans. In fact, Pan-Germanism itself is a coalition of coalitions in the most literal sense of the word. Germany, Austria, Hungary, the Balkans, Turkey, are none of them states where the racial lines have been unified, the religious antipathies even minimized, and the state or administration able to rely upon the support and affection of the whole people. Out of such material, Pan-Germanism proposes to create another confederation, whose basis will be even more slender than that of any of the confederations out of which it is to be made, and whose continued existence will necessarily be daily exposed to the assaults of internal enemies. A vital change in any one of the confederations composing it would in all probability have fatal effect upon the greater entity.

It is not too much to say that the success of the whole scheme depends absolutely upon the stability and efficiency of Germany and Austria.

Nay, the continuance even of the attempt to execute the scheme is contingent upon the continuance in office of those who are at present directing the policy of those states and upon their ability to dictate the disposition of the national resources. The continuity of policy is an absolutely indispensable part of Pan-Germanism; yet there are no countries in Europe where the forces struggling to effect fundamental alterations in constitutional, administrative, and political conditions, are more persistent and more powerful, and which possess greater chances of success. The number of irreconcilables, which means to the European the number of those who regard the very existence of the state as a fundamental grievance which nothing except its destruction can remedy, is very large, and comprises considerable sections of the population, who occupy important strategic positions, and who elect without difficulty numerous representatives to the assemblies. The Socialists in Germany are exceedingly strong, are growing in numbers at a portentous rate, and are rapidly outstripping the other parties in the Prussian houses and in the Reichstag; they already practically control the city of Berlin and comprise the numerical majority in many other cities. The Opposition in the Austrian and Hungarian Parliaments is so strong that the business of the session frequently has to be suspended for days and weeks, and it has more than once been necessary to break the deadlock by calling in the military to remove the obstructionists, before any business could be done. The system of representation, provided by the constitutions of these nations, permits most of the people to vote, but evaluates the individual vote on the basis of property and education. The adoption of universal suffrage of the English, French, or American pattern would promptly throw into a hopeless minority the parties which now control those states and practically reverse their policies in every particular. The official proclamation of the Socialist Party in Germany declares the present aggressive stand of Germany wrong. It is perhaps not without significance that the most popular party in Germany takes upon the question of Pan-Germanism the attitude of the irreconcilable, and, because it involves war, declares the very nature of the scheme inexpedient and undesirable. All of these influences may not actually be powerful enough to prevent the present rulers from making the nominal alliances which will put Pan-Germanism in the arena, but it is scarcely probable that they will not have an exceedingly important effect upon its stability and its continuity of policy. That Pan-Germanism can be created is not

perhaps to be gainsaid; that such a confederation could perhaps inflict a crushing blow upon
the Triple Entente is quite within the bounds
of probability; but that Pan-Germanism, resting
upon such a basis, can long withstand the assault
of its internal and external enemies seems utterly
improbable.

The greatest genius of the English has been
their skill in diplomacy, the keenness with which
they have ordinarily analyzed the situation, and
the great ability they have shown in expounding
its various possibilities to the disorderly elements
in Europe. They have won their present position,
as the English historians have forcibly pointed
out, by taking advantage of the mutual jealousies
and rivalries of Europe. Time and time again a
great coalition has been actually put into the field
against them, only to be rent apart by English
diplomacy. The Germans assume that the possibility of repeating such feats of diplomacy has
been dissipated by the alterations in the political structure of Germany, Austria, and Italy, or
by the reduction of England's relative strength.
Yet, it is far from true that England is isolated
in the world; she possesses three immensely powerful allies in France, Russia, and the United
States; that coalition already holds in its hands
the greater part of the habitable globe, and con-

trols the oceans, the major part of the economic resources of the entire world, and practically its whole financial fabric. The fundamental error Germany has committed has been to suppose, that because the position of England in the world is vitally altered, because England can no longer be maintained in her proud predominance by the factors which originally created it, that there are no factors of prime importance to maintain it. The truth seems to be that the English position has been changed in nature but not in essence. Because she does not rely upon factors to-day which were conclusive in their effect upon European politics three centuries ago, their present worthlessness must not be construed as the total absence of all strength. In this particular, however, nothing is changed. The condition of Europe itself, in which English diplomacy has so invariably found weapons for the defense of the island kingdom, to-day presents to as great a degree as ever before a tangle of conflicting interests and traditional antipathies, in which the English are more than likely in their habitual manner to find the solution for their present difficulties. If it is true that England's strength has been due to the balance of power in Europe rather than to her own physical resources, the prime condition for the continuance of her authority is still in existence.

CHAPTER XVII

THE PROBABILITY OF THE SUCCESS OF PAN-GERMANISM

II. External Weaknesses

WHEN the Germans prate of the willingness of the world to join them in the hope of looting the British Empire, they seem to suppose that the English and the French will tamely sit still and allow them to bring their plans to perfection. Something has already been said in a previous chapter about Italy's position in the Mediterranean, her fear of Austria, and, in general, her lack of that same vital interest in Pan-Germanism which her two allies undoubtedly possess. While the great scheme is probably the most plausible and feasible ever suggested for the preservation and expansion of Germany and Austria, there are many other possibilities before Italy. She has already proved in the case of the Tripolitan War that she has her price and is by no means bound to the Triple Alliance with eternal chains. Suppose now that England and France should increase their offer to her and should be able to fulfill it, would she still cling to

Pan-Germanism, and could it be completed without her assistance and with her opposition? Suppose France offered Spain a part of Morocco; that England offered Italy Egypt in addition to Tripoli, reserving only the right of free passage through the Suez Canal and the control of the Red Sea; that the Triple Entente guaranteed the autonomy of Greece and the Balkan States, and secured from Russia the suspension at least of her claims to territorial expansion in that district, in exchange for at least the right of free passage through the Straits and the control of the Black Sea; suppose that they offered the Young Turks control of Asia Minor, with financial support for their government, in exchange for the commercial privileges of the Baghdad Railway and the right to irrigate Mesopotamia; suppose England and Russia offered the Persians autonomy in exchange for a monopoly of trade and the right to construct the Trans-Persian Railway; would not the situation be materially altered? Would not the Triple Entente be more than likely to assure itself of the permanent support of these states whose adherence is absolutely essential to Pan-Germanism? Would the Pan-German Confederation, even if actually created, be proof against such offers, when the Triple Entente could without exaggeration promise to every one of those states such privileges as the price of their support, with the certainty that their desertion would so completely destroy the confederation and weaken Germany and Austria as to make actual war impossible? Truth to tell, the Triple Entente would prefer to keep all it has; but is it not a purely gratuitous assumption to suppose that they will be so blind as not to see that by parting with some of it they might easily insure their possession of the remainder for another couple of generations?

While the Germans have correctly read the history of the British Empire and have appreciated to the full the importance of the assistance of the native races in creating the present position held by England, they seem to believe that the English power at present has no other basis than that which it possessed in the beginning. They forget the ability with which the English have ruled India, the undeniable benefits which they have conferred upon the Hindu, the fact that the common people have for the first time been treated with what we should call decency, accorded justice, and allowed to retain a sufficient proportion of their produce to live upon. However true may be the tales of oppression in India that Germany and Russia have industriously collected and spread, they are certainly insignificant compared to the oppression and suffering visited upon that unhappy land since before the time when history was. The wave of democracy, which is sweeping on into the Orient, has not escaped the Hindus; but a most careful investigation of the question by disinterested students has yet failed to reveal any very considerable number of Hindus who believe the varied races huddled together in India capable of governing themselves. The English have appreciated (and so far as we can tell with absolute justice) the fact that the democratic movement in India is the work of one race and one religion, which would be glad to rule over the other races and the other religions. It is not, therefore, difficult to demonstrate to the Hindu of the Brahmin caste the undesirability of being ruled by the Mohammedans, while the latter are by no means enthusiastic about being ruled by the Brahmin. Each is zealous about obtaining for his own sect the right to govern India; each is as unwilling to be ruled by other Hindu sects, who do not agree with him in religion, as he is to have the present English rule continued. When it is simple to demonstrate to them all that the departure of the English will certainly not result in the government of India by any native race or sect, but in its conquest by Russia or Germany, the desire of the Hindus and Mohammedans for the expulsion of the English is necessarily much modified. So clear have the English made these facts to those natives who alone are capable, either from their ability or from their position, of undertaking such a movement, that the likelihood of any revolt against the English in India is small and the faithful support of the native princes firmly assured, at any rate, so long as the present international situation continues. Suppose that the international situation should suddenly change, that, for any one of fifty reasons, the expulsion of all foreigners from India should seem probable, would not the English then be in a position to offer the natives, in exchange for the trade monopoly they have always had and to which the native does not apparently seriously object, their assistance in securing and maintaining actual autonomy? Would not the Germans or the Russians be met by a very different sort of a force than the beggarly thousands of Englishmen whom they affect so to despise? In fact, to snatch India from a few thousand Englishmen with the assistance of the Hindu is one thing; to conquer India from the English and the Hindu combined, in the face of a century of admirable administration by England and the promise of practical autonomy for the native states in the future, would be a very different thing. If one is eminently feasible, the other is exceedingly improbable; and the facts of the situation, so far as they can be learned, seem to indicate with precision that the latter is the truth.

The Germans have made much of the lack of common economic interests between England and her self-governing colonies because of the distances which sunder them. As a matter of fact, it is easier to-day to carry on trade with New Zealand at a distance of over twelve thousand miles — it is possible to send that distance commodities that until the last half-century were never shipped at all — than it was before the year 1850 to carry on trade overland between Berlin and Munich. Nor are the freight charges in one case probably much in excess of those in the other. Certainly the time consumed does not so greatly differ. Most people forget with ease the common facts of history concerning the length of time consumed by journeys undertaken without the aid of the railway. While the analogy must not be too closely pressed, it is substantially true that the economic tie between England and her colonies is probably quite as close to-day as the economic ties between different parts of the German Empire previous to the Zollverein. To be sure, this argument does not presage great strength for such relations, but it does show that the mere fact of the existence of the Atlantic

Ocean is not sufficient to prove that there is not and never can be a substantial identity of economic interests. But waiving that, assuming that the only bond there is or can be between England and her self-governing colonies is that of blood, it will be difficult for the student to deny that the racial tie is more than likely to be sufficient to hold the Empire together, and to secure actual support from the colonies in ships and troops. Enthusiastic response to the recent appeal of the mother country for assistance shows conclusively that there is a good deal more likelihood of the tie between England and her colonies being sufficient to hold them together than that the present political tie will be sufficient to prevent the complete dismemberment of Austria-Hungary. If we take the most unfavorable statement possible of the British Empire and the most favorable statement of the actual situation in the Dual Monarchy, it will be difficult to deny that the British Empire possesses all those qualities of unity of race, of language, of religion, of economic interest, of policy, of loyalty, which the Dual Monarchy conspicuously lacks. And the continued existence of the Dual Monarchy is a good deal more important to Pan-Germanism than the assistance of the English colonies is likely to be to the Triple Entente.

In regard to the economic weapons upon which Germany places so much reliance, the truth of the facts alleged is not possible of denial, but the inferences drawn from them seem to be enormously exaggerated. Unquestionably, Germany does possess the reality, and other nations possess paper evidences of their investments, and if Germany should decline to pay her loans, and if she should be able to maintain herself in war, disastrous results might be produced. The possibility of the confiscation of the English investments in other parts of the world does not seem to be probable. It has always been true that the strong man could rob the weaker, that the strong nation could rob the smaller; but the experience of men throughout the centuries seems to have demonstrated pretty effectively, that, even when the thief is not punished by the arm of justice, there are economic laws which somehow seem to prevent the attainment of the degree of benefit he expected to derive. So radical a disavowal of the strength of the feeling in favor of commercial and national honesty is far removed from the general opinion of the financial world, and it seems probable that the Germans have very much underestimated the strength of the moral obligation which binds the commercial world together.

EXTERNAL WEAKNESSES

Above all, this talk of confiscation as a last resort, of taking possession for nothing of Germany's development, is all based upon the supposition that it will be as easy to keep it as it is to get it, and upon the equally peculiar notion that the financial situation will remain what it was some years ago when these notions were first promulgated. They are no longer secret, nor have the foreign investors failed to take account of the fact that, even should Germany take no steps to repudiate her debts, the coming of war would for the time being at any rate rob them of their incomes. They are not investing to-day at the rate they did before in German securities; they will no longer advance loans to the German and Austrian Governments without pledges in regard to the destination of the money of such a nature as to make treachery improbable; they have already been at work for some years exchanging their investments in Germany for other securities. American investors are inclined to greet such a supposition as repudiation with incredulity, and the small European investor, who is not informed in the details of current politics, is apt to suppose that the German or Austrian Government is necessarily trustworthy; but the great financial heads do not seem to be of that opinion. An Austrian war loan, offered in De-

cember, 1912, at 97, was not subscribed with
alacrity. None of the Germans seem to remember
that after the war is over, after they have succeeded in destroying France and robbing England,
they will be forced to have relations with the rest
of the world and with each other. The effect of
the wholesale repudiation of their debts, private
and national, however crushing it might be at
the moment to their creditors, and whether or
not it was intentional or involuntary, would
almost certainly react upon themselves in the
future so unfavorably as to render the whole
operation scarcely to their advantage. With such
a record, how could they expect to obtain the
confidence of the Hindu and of the Chinese, to
say nothing of maintaining that belief in each
other's honesty and faithfulness upon which the
whole structure of Pan-Germanism rests?

Their economic weapons, about which the
Germans talk so glibly, the starving of England,
the depriving her factories of raw materials, the
cutting-off of her supplies for the maintenance of
a fleet, these depend one and all upon the ability
of the German navy to outmanœuvre the English
and get possession of the Channel in such fashion
that a pitched battle would be necessary to dis-
lodge it, or upon its ability to defeat the English
fleet in the first place in so decisive a manner that

assistance could not come from the Mediterranean and from America in time to avert the catastrophe. It is perhaps well to remember in this connection that the Germans are not a nation of sailors, and that their navy has thus far been used only for manœuvres like those of the King of France when he marched up the hill and then marched down again. It is true, as the Germans say in defense, that the English have never used the present type of ship in actual warfare; but it is surely exceedingly important to remember that the English invented and designed the present type of ship, and in all probability know more about its use than the Germans are likely to. The latter seem to lay more stress upon the size of their fleet than they do upon its efficiency, and seem to suppose that, if it were more numerous than the English, victory would be assured. The Spanish Armada, to cite one familiar example from many, was reputed at the time to be so powerful, and certainly did so largely outnumber the English fleet, that Europeans supposed no resistance would be possible; yet in this action, as in many others, the English demonstrated conclusively that knowledge of seamanship and the efficiency of the individual vessel was of vastly more consequence than numbers. While at the present day there is no great sailor of conspicuous

fame in the English navy, it is difficult to believe
that the nation, which produced in moments
of danger men like Drake, Blake, and Nelson,
would be incapable in a similar crisis of producing
as suddenly from the ranks some man of equally
conspicuous talent. It will be early enough to
assume the defeat of the English on the sea when
that event occurs.

The German army is probably more efficient
than the fleet, but is very likely not as efficient
as the Germans think it is. Military critics have
declared it bound too tightly with red tape, filled
with unintelligent officials, too stiff and mechan-
ical in its evolutions to give much of an account
of itself in battle. Certainly, it cannot compare
in point of size with the army Russia could put
in the field, and competent judges have declared
it far inferior in quality to the French army. To
be sure, none of these armies have recently been
under fire except the Russian army, whose experience was perhaps not a desirable preparation for
another war. The condition of the English army
in England is admitted on all sides to be bad,
though the actual deficiencies have no doubt
been exaggerated by the eager advocates of universal conscription. But while the Anglo-Saxon
race has invariably not shown to advantage in the
field before the war, nor indeed during the first

years of a long war, they have usually won. From the point of view of strategy, the Duke of Wellington was hopelessly beaten at Waterloo; according to all the rules of tacticians, his thin line of redcoats could never hold such a position; but the critics have since been compelled to admit that the English soldiers possessed some qualities, which other troops did not have, that enabled them to hold that position despite the odds and win one of the decisive battles of history. No doubt all Anglo-Saxons are prejudiced, but they will not credit the supposition that the descendants of the men who fought Napoleon and the men themselves who won the war in South Africa, when they meet an invader upon their own soil, will be unable to give a satisfactory account of themselves.

The really doubtful factor in the present situation is Russia. She, far more than England, holds the scale. She is likely to gain in the long run whichever side wins. Should Germany overthrow England and France in Europe and take possession of the Mediterranean, Russia would certainly reach India first. If she should join Germany, the downfall of England and France would be assured, and the victors could divide the world at their leisure. But she could not join Germany without renouncing her ambitions in the Baltic, without permitting the Germans to overrun that sea and throwing herself back upon Asia and making it the centre of a new empire. The likelihood of such a renunciation of her position in Europe is exceedingly small. The probability that Germans would believe in her sincerity, if she offered them an alliance on such a basis, is infinitely smaller. Germany is so exposed that the treachery of Russia would be fatal. As the situation looks at present, nothing short of the breaking of the alliance between England, France, the United States, and Russia can permit the German scheme to obtain anything more than a temporary and partial success. The first three of these allies cannot leave the alliance without endangering everything they hold dear. The fourth can do so only by the renunciation of ambitions which have been the very backbone of Russian policy ever since Russia herself emerged upon the plane of European politics.

THE END

APPENDIX